D1470113

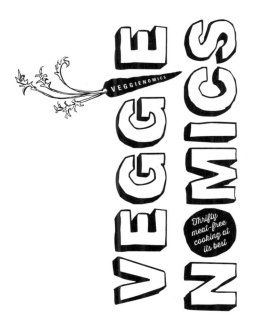

VEGGIENOMICS

VEGGIE NOMICS

Thrifty meat-free cooking at its best

VEGGIENOMICS

Thrifty meat-free cooking at its best

★ *Nicola Graimes* ★

NOURISH

EAT WELL, LIVE WELL

Veggienomics

Nicola Graimes

First published in the USA and Canada in 2014 by
Nourish, an imprint of Watkins Publishing Limited
PO Box 883, Oxford, OX1 9PL, UK

A member of Osprey Group

Osprey Publishing
PO Box 3985
New York, NY 10185-3985
Tel: (001) 212 753 4402
Email: info@ospreypublishing.com

Publisher: Grace Cheetham
Project Manager: Rebecca Woods
Editor: Liz Jones
Managing Designer: Suzanne Tuhrim
Commissioned photography: Toby Scott
Food Stylist: Jayne Cross
Prop Stylist: Lucy Harvey
Illustrator: Cecilia Carey
Production: Uzma Taj

ISBN: 978-1-84899-194-1

10 9 8 7 6 5 4 3 2 1

Typeset in Block Dog, Thirsty Rough and Univers
Color reproduction by PDQ, UK
Printed in China

Notes on the Recipes

Unless otherwise stated:

- Use medium eggs, fruit and vegetables
- Use fresh ingredients, including herbs and spices
- Do not mix metric and US measurements
- 1 tsp. = 5ml   1 tbsp. = 15ml   1 cup = 240ml

Publisher's Note

While every care has been taken in compiling the
recipes for this book, Watkins Publishing Limited,
or any other persons who have been involved
in working on this publication, cannot accept
responsibility for any errors or omissions,
inadvertent or not, that may be found in the recipes
or text, nor for any problems that may arise as
a result of preparing one of these recipes. If you
are pregnant or breastfeeding or have any special
dietary requirements or medical conditions, it is
advisable to consult a medical professional before
following any of the recipes contained in this book.

Watkins Publishing Limited is supporting the
Woodland Trust, the UK's leading woodland
conservation charity, by funding tree-planting
initiatives and woodland maintenance.

www.nourishbooks.com

Contents

Introduction

In my previous cookbook, *New Vegetarian Kitchen*, the focus was on experimenting with cooking techniques and ingredients in an adventurous way; playing around with flavors, colors and textures to create a collection of contemporary recipes that utilize the amazing range of foods now available to us. *Veggienomics* pares things back with a series of recipes that are in tune with the demands of today's home cook: straightforward, simple dishes that don't compromise on good taste, are nutritious and, importantly, don't burn a hole in your pocket.

We are all increasingly aware of the price of food and the environmental cost and inefficiencies of producing meat on a large scale, which is why cooking vegetarian—whether 100 percent or the occasional meal—makes both economic and environmental sense. Additionally, most of us don't have much time to spend shopping or cooking on a daily basis. *Veggienomics* helps you to plan ahead (making the most of what you've got is crucial when you're on a budget), with advice on shopping, stocking the pantry, making the most of your freezer, using up leftovers, menu planning, growing your own fresh produce and even foraging for free.

Here is a collection of recipes that make use of cooking staples such as beans, legumes, pasta, rice, noodles and grains as well as nuts, cheese, dairy and eggs, supplemented with fresh vegetables —be they store-bought, homegrown or foraged.

I've taken a back-to-basics approach, with recipes for making your own stock, spice mix, cream cheese, yogurt, preserves, pickles and syrups, as well as sprouting your own beans. These aren't just fun and easy to do, but they also make economic sense—these foods can be pricey to buy. Some figures suggest that in the West we throw away as much as a third of the food we buy—which is why it makes sense to make the most of the food we have by using the freezer, and cooking with leftovers (even just a crust of bread, cheese rind or some surplus cooked veg).

Geared to our busy lives and varying culinary demands, each chapter in the book includes recipes and suggestions for snacks, lunches and dinners. There are also suggestions for matching recipes if you are cooking a whole meal. Where a recipe uses a slightly more unusual ingredient, an alternative is given in case you can't find it. I also like to use the same ingredient in a few recipes so you aren't left with a bottle of something languishing in the cupboard.

My original plan for *Veggienomics* centered around clever shopping and making the most of the weekly trip to the grocery store, but then it blossomed into something wider to include growing your own fresh produce and foraging, both favorite pastimes of mine. This book isn't about living off the land big style—rather it is intended to give you a taste of what's feasible from a small plot, or by discovering your local environment.

I wouldn't say I'm a big-time gardener, but I like to grow a selection of veg and herbs at home and share a garden plot with a few friends, where we have had a good rate of success. It's not only immensely satisfying, but also extremely therapeutic when you otherwise spend much of your time in front of a computer. Similarly, my interest in foraging was initially spurred on after finding some spectacular porcini mushrooms—it doesn't get much better than that!

So if you want to cut down on the amount of meat you eat on a weekly basis (or even cut it out of your diet altogether), and watch what you spend on your grocery bill, I hope that you will agree that *Veggienomics* includes recipes to inspire … without costing a fortune.

STOCKING THE PANTRY

Pantry ingredients form the cornerstone of the recipes. You'll find that you have the foundations of many good meals, and only have to buy the fresh ingredients to supplement them.

If you eat pasta, rice, beans and lentils on a weekly basis it makes economic sense to buy them in bulk. If you don't eat them regularly enough to buy large quantities for yourself, share large bags with family and friends. It's also possible to buy some dried foods in loose form, meaning you can buy exactly the amount you need and don't have to pay for fancy packaging.

Rice and Grains

A staple food for over half the world's population, rice features in many cuisines: think Italian risotto, Spanish paella and Middle Eastern pilafs, not forgetting Asian food.

The two main ways to cook rice are the open boiling method, where you cover the rice with plenty of water, then drain it when cooked, and the absorption method. I tend to go for the latter, as taught to me by the rice connoisseur Sri Owen, as I find it gives perfectly cooked, fluffy rice.

To cook long-grain rice for four people by the absorption method, thoroughly rinse 1 cup rice to remove excess starch. Put the rice in a saucepan and cover with 2 cups water and ½ teaspoon salt (the water should be about ½ inch above the top of the rice). Bring to a boil, uncovered, then turn the heat down to its lowest setting, cover with a lid and simmer 10 minutes, or until the water has been absorbed and the rice is tender. Remove the pan from the heat and let stand, covered, 5 minutes. Fluff up the grains with a fork before serving.

While rice, in its many forms, reigns supreme in the world of grains, there are so many more types to choose from when stocking a pantry: barley, bulgur, couscous, buckwheat, oats, polenta and quinoa are all worthy of mention and inexpensive. Barley is great in hearty soups and stews, and also makes a good alternative to rice in risotto and paella. I like to use protein-rich quinoa, or buckwheat, bulgur or couscous, to serve with tagines and stews as well as in salads and pilafs. Polenta and oats make a lovely crispy crust for fritters, croquettes and burgers.

Pasta and Noodles

Long or short, thick or thin, smooth or ridged, curly or straight—there is a plethora of shapes and sizes of dried pasta to choose from. The choice may feel intimidating, but the general "rule" is that the pasta shape should work in harmony with the accompanying sauce. Perfect pasta pairings include thin, long pasta such as spaghetti and linguine with olive oil-based sauces, and thicker strands with cream and tomato sauces, while heavy, chunky sauces require a sturdier, shorter shape such as rigatoni or penne. Ridged or curly shapes are good for "capturing" sauces, giving them something to cling on to. It makes sense to have a varied selection—but then again you don't want too many open bags, containing not enough pasta to make a decent-sized meal!

When cooking pasta, immerse it (a decent serving is 1 heaped cup dried pasta per person) in plenty of boiling water to prevent it sticking. Salt the water generously (about 1 tablespoon per 4 cups); the water should be as salty as the sea. Stir the pasta occasionally to prevent it sticking, and keep the water at a rolling boil. When draining pasta, reserve a little of the cooking water to loosen the accompanying sauce, if necessary.

While noodles also come in a range of lengths and thicknesses, it tends to be the type of grain used, rather than the shape, that defines how they are cooked and served. Egg noodles and chunky udon work in stir-fries, while lighter rice and soba noodles suit soupy broths and Asian salads.

Beans and Lentils

Dried beans and lentils are essential staples in my kitchen. Extremely economical and nutritious, it pays to buy them in bulk if they are a regular part of your diet. Look for smooth, plump dried beans, and store them in an airtight container in a cool, dark cupboard where they'll keep best up to a year. Keep an eye on the use-by date, as beans become tough when old.

Don't dismiss canned beans and lentils, as they make a convenient addition to the pantry for when you don't have time or the inclination to soak and cook dried ones. I like to use them in speedy lunchtime salads or warming pan-fries and, as they tend to be softer in texture than cooked dried beans, they are great in pâtés, stuffings, croquettes and fritters.

The relevant recipes in this book give the cup measures of both drained canned beans and dried cooked beans. A standard 15-ounce can of chickpeas will contain both the chickpeas and brine, so you need to keep an eye on the drained weight given on the label: for instance, a 15-ounce can will contain a scant 1⅔ cups chickpeas (about 9 ounces).

Back to dried beans. With a few exceptions they will cook more quickly and evenly if pre-soaked 6 to 8 hours in plenty of cold water. If time is short, you can try the quick-soak method: cook the beans in boiling water 2 minutes, then remove the pan from the heat, cover and leave 1 hour until cold.

Whichever method you use, drain and rinse them before cooking. Dried lentils and mung beans don't need pre-soaking, but you should rinse them well before cooking.

To cook dried beans and lentils, put them in a pan and cover with plenty of cold water, cover, and bring to a boil. (If cooking dried kidney beans it is essential that you first boil them vigorously 10 minutes to destroy the toxins.) Turn the heat down, part-cover the pan and gently boil, stirring occasionally, until the beans are tender. Salt the cooking water about three quarters of the way through cooking to avoid toughening the beans. Also, check the pan occasionally to make sure there is enough water and top up if necessary. Cooking times will vary depending on the age of the beans or lentils, but use the following table as a guideline (a pressure cooker will reduce the time by around three quarters).

	Pre-soaking	Cooking time
BEANS		
Aduki beans	yes	45 minutes
Black beans	yes	1 to 1½ hours
Cannellini beans	yes	1 to 1½ hours
Chickpeas	yes	1 to 2 hours
Cranberry beans	yes	1 to 1½ hours
Fava (broad) beans (split)	yes	40 minutes to 1 hour
Flageolet beans	yes	1 to 1½ hours
Kidney beans	yes	1½ hours
Lima (butter) beans	yes	1 hour
Mung beans	no	45 minutes
Navy beans	yes	1 to 1½ hours
Pinto beans	yes	1 to 1½ hours
Soybeans	yes	2 to 3 hours
LENTILS		
Green lentils	no	30 minutes to 45 minutes
French (Puy) lentils	no	30 minutes to 45 minutes
Red split lentils	no	25 minutes

FILLING THE REFRIGERATOR

Much of the food that tends to be thrown away is chilled, so it pays to be mindful when stocking the refrigerator to avoid waste. When shopping for food, take a list (with a rough breakdown of the week's meals)—this will help to keep you focused and avoid making unwanted impulse purchases that won't be used. To ensure that chilled foods last as long as they should, store them correctly in the refrigerator. Make sure your refrigerator is energy efficient and set at 40–41°F, and be conscious of "best by" or "eat by" dates. Make sure food is wrapped or covered to avoid cross-contamination and the transfer of smells from strong cheese, garlic or scallions, for instance. Many say that eggs don't have to be stored in the refrigerator if you have a cool place to keep them, but when the weather is warm, it's sensible to put them in the door of the refrigerator. Similarly, the bottom of the refrigerator or the salad drawer are the perfect temperature for uncooked vegetables and salad greens.

USING THE FREEZER

Freezing is a useful way to preserve food, extending its shelf-life and enabling you to make the most of leftovers. Make meals in bulk and freeze the surplus. Also, leftover crusts of bread are perfect for turning into breadcrumbs and freezing in containers—you can use them right from frozen.

A full freezer costs less to run than a half-empty one, so it pays to make the most of the space, but remember that food that is past its best is not improved by freezing. Keep the freezer at 0°F or below, as at this temperature food pathogens and harmful micro-organisms are dormant. For best results, freeze home-cooked foods on the super-freeze setting. Quick-frozen foods have smaller ice crystals, which means they thaw without losing moisture and nutrients.

Freeze soups, stews and sauces in portions, so you can defrost the right amount when needed. Leftover wine, stock and chopped herbs (immersed in a little water) can be frozen in ice cube trays, then transferred to a ziploc freezer bag. Make the most of precious freezer space by freezing stews and sauces flat in thick freezer bags. Plastic containers with tight-fitting lids are useful, too; try empty, well-washed yogurt cartons, margarine containers and take-out cartons.

"Tray-freezing" is an ideal way to freeze fruit and vegetables as well as vegetarian sausage rolls, burgers, pastries, patties and pies to keep them separate and prevent them sticking together during freezing. When frozen, transfer them to an appropriate-sized bag or container. Wrap individual items in plastic wrap first to keep them separate. If freezing your own food, make sure it has cooled down, as warm foods raise the internal temperature of the freezer and could affect other foods. It's a good idea to write the name, portion size and date of freezing—or be super-efficient and keep a record of the contents of your freezer so things don't get forgotten about.

Defrost foods at room temperature (about 65°F) or in the refrigerator if time allows. You can also defrost foods in the microwave or oven, but this may affect their texture. Last but not least, avoid re-freezing previously defrosted food.

GROW-YOUR-OWN

I'm relatively new to the world of vegetable growing. Over the years I've had some success growing veg in my small patio garden, in pots, grow-bags and beds, and have had an herb garden for as long as I can remember, but I've recently joined forces with a few friends on a garden plot and we've been rewarded with a bounteous supply of fresh produce. An increasing number of people have gotten hooked on growing their own fresh fruit and vegetables, but if it's not for you, then the next best thing is a local box delivery service or farmers' market.

The grow-your-own tips in *Veggienomics* arm you with the basics and focus on the fresh produce that I've grown myself. Unfortunately, there was not enough space to go into much detail (which is why I haven't gone into seed varieties) but hopefully I've given you enough to inspire you to try growing your own veg, as well as highlighting any planting idiosyncrasies. If you do have a glut of vegetables, they freeze well, but it's best to blanch and refresh them before freezing as then they tend to keep better. Alternatively, freeze them uncooked, but do cook them soon after defrosting.

If you intend to preserve your homegrown produce (or indeed foraging finds) by turning it into jams, jellies, chutneys or pickles, you must sterilize the jars you intend to use first to avoid contamination and spoilage. This is easy to do, but it's vital to pay careful attention to hygiene. Wash new or reused jars (removing any labels first) well in hot soapy water, then rinse and put them on a baking tray in a cold oven. Turn the oven to 350°F and, once it has reached this temperature, leave the jars in the oven 10 minutes. Use new lids, rather than reusing the old ones, and sterilize them first by boiling them in a pan of water 10 minutes. Carefully remove with tongs and let dry. Can your preserves when they are still warm and cover with the lids. You may have to tighten the lids as they cool.

FOOD FOR FREE

Foraging is immensely pleasurable—there is little more rewarding than finding edible delights that are absolutely free. It's a great way to get in touch with the seasons, as well as discovering that many of the so-called "weeds" you've walked past for years are actually edible plants—and taste good, too.

Many of the recipes in this book contain wild foods: from coastal vegetables, flowers and nuts to herbs, mushrooms and greens, yet my selection just scratches the surface of what can be found. This taste of foraging will hopefully inspire you to go out and gather, if you haven't already done so. Be respectful of nature when foraging, do not uproot plants or pick greedily, and also make sure the plants you are picking aren't a protected species. A good foraging book is a must for identifying wild foods, and is imperative when looking for fungi. It will help you discover the edible wonders of the countryside and coastline—and cities can be surprisingly fruitful, too.

Basics and Accompaniments

The purpose of this eclectic collection of recipes is two-fold:
some of the recipes form the foundation of dishes contained
within the main chapters, while others are accompaniments
that will embellish and enhance meals. For instance, no kitchen
should be without a good, staple vegetable stock recipe.
It is the base for many recipes in the book and can be stored
in portions in the freezer. At the other end of the scale is the
Korean condiment, kimchi, a potent pickle relish that's great
with Asian dishes, pies or cheese platters. There are also
useful recipes for thick plain yogurt, pastry dough, spice mixes
and salsas, and don't miss trying the Quick Preserved Lemons.

This makes a basic, light unsweetened pastry dough, which is ideal for lining and topping quiches and pies. For a richer pastry dough, you could add an egg to the dough and reduce the milk to 1 to 2 tablespoons. For a sweet dough, stir in scant ⅓ cup sugar at the end of Step 1. The dough is made by hand, but you can use a food processor instead.

Pastry Dough

Makes: *enough to line an 11-inch quiche dish*   **Preparation time:** *10 minutes, plus 30 minutes chilling*

1¾ cups all-purpose flour
a pinch of salt

½ cup (1 stick) cold butter, cut into small, even-sized pieces
about ¼ cup milk

1. Sift the flour and salt into a bowl, stir until combined, then add the butter. Lightly rub in the butter with your fingertips until the mixture resembles fine breadcrumbs.

2. Gradually stir in the milk until the crumbs start to come together, then knead briefly into a smooth ball of dough. Wrap in plastic wrap, press into a disc and chill 30 minutes in the refrigerator until ready to use.

Uncooked pastry dough can be frozen up to 3 months. Put the disc or sheet of dough in a freezer-proof bag and freeze in a wax paper-lined baking tray before transferring to a ziploc freezer bag.

This recipe is a general guide, as you can make stock from any vegetables you have at hand. Root vegetables make a good starting point, but avoid using too much of one type as it will dominate the flavor. Salt isn't added to the stock, as you will probably be using the stock in another recipe, and a salt-less stock will enable you to control how salty the final dish is.

Vegetable Stock

Makes: *7½ cups*   **Preparation time:** *10 minutes*
Cooking time: *1 hour 10 minutes*

2 tablespoons olive oil
2 onions, chopped
2 leeks, chopped
3 celery stalks, chopped
3 carrots, chopped
1 turnip, chopped

3 garlic cloves, peeled and crushed
6 parsley sprigs
2 bay leaves
1 small handful of thyme sprigs
½ teaspoon peppercorns

1. Heat the oil in a large, heavy pot over medium heat. Add the vegetables and cook 10 minutes, part-covered, and stirring occasionally, until softened. Stir in the garlic, parsley, bay leaves, thyme and peppercorns.

2. Pour in 7½ cups water and bring to a boil, then turn the heat down and simmer over low heat 1 hour. Strain the stock, discard the solids and let cool. Keep in the refrigerator up to 1 week or freeze in portions.

This forms the base of Asian soups, curries and stir-fries.

Asian Stock

Makes: *about 5 cups*   **Preparation time:** *10 minutes, plus making the stock and 1 hour infusing*   **Cooking time:** *10 minutes*

⅔ recipe quantity Vegetable Stock (opposite)
2 lemongrass stalks, bruised
1 long cinnamon stick
2 star anise

6 cardamom pods, split
6 cloves
2-inch piece of ginger root, sliced
    into thin rounds

1. Put the stock, lemongrass, cinnamon, star anise, cardamom, cloves and ginger in a large pot and bring to a boil, then turn the heat down and simmer, part-covered, 10 minutes. Remove from the heat and let infuse 1 hour. Use as instructed, or let cool and then chill or freeze.

This aromatic blend of spices works well in both coconut-based and tomato-based Indian curries. Keep any unused spice mix in a jar covered with a lid and store in a cool, dark place.

Curry Spice Mix

Makes: *enough for 4 curries*   **Preparation time:** *10 minutes*
Cooking time: *2 minutes*

2 tablespoons coriander seeds
2 teaspoons cumin seeds
2 tablespoons fenugreek seeds
12 cardamom pods, seeds removed

1 teaspoon cloves
4 dried red chilies
2 teaspoons turmeric
1 teaspoon ground cinnamon

1. Put the coriander, cumin, fenugreek and cardamom seeds in a large, dry skillet. Add the cloves and chilies and toast 1 to 2 minutes over medium-low heat, shaking the pan occasionally, until the spices smell aromatic and slightly toasted.

2. Tip the spices into a mortar and, using a pestle, grind to a powder, or use a spice grinder. Stir in the turmeric and cinnamon and store in a covered jar in a cool, dark place.

Rich, creamy, delicious and much cheaper than store-bought, you don't need a special yogurt maker to make this, but a kitchen thermometer is recommended. It's also important to be scrupulous about hygiene and make sure all your equipment is clean to avoid contamination. Depending on the time of year, you may need to consider how to keep the yogurt warm while it cultures. It's obviously much easier when it's warm, but in the winter months it helps if you have a thermos flask or use a gas oven with just the pilot light on. For a lighter, lowfat yogurt, use 2% milk instead and omit the cream.

Wholemilk Yogurt

Makes: *about 4 cups*   **Preparation time:** *55 minutes, plus 8 hours cooling and fermenting*   **Cooking time:** *25 minutes*

4 cups whole milk, preferably organic
¼ cup heavy cream
¼ cup plain live or bio yogurt

1. Slowly warm the milk in a large, heavy pan over medium-low heat, stirring occasionally, until bubbles start to appear on the surface; it should read 185°F on the thermometer. Once the milk has reached this heat, keep it there about 20 minutes, or until it has reduced by a quarter, stirring occasionally. You may need to turn the heat down to low during this time.

2. Turn the heat off, remove any skin that has formed on the surface of the milk and stir in the cream. Let the mixture cool to 110°F, stirring occasionally. This usually takes around 40 to 45 minutes.

3. Put the live yogurt in a 4-cup sterilized Mason jar (see page 11) and pour in a quarter of the milk mixture. Stir until combined, then add the remaining milk mixture and stir again. Fasten the lid and wrap in plastic wrap, then a towel, then a black plastic bag to keep the warmth in. Leave in a warm place, ideally around 104°F, 5 to 8 hours or until thickened. Stir well and chill in the refrigerator until ready to eat. It will keep up to 1 week.

To make the most delicious cream cheese, stir 1 teaspoon sea salt into the yogurt, then drain in a jelly bag or a cheesecloth-lined strainer overnight in the refrigerator to remove the whey.

If you like the idea of making cheese, then a simple, drained curd cheese is the perfect starting point—it's easy and requires no special equipment or ingredients. Paneer is a delicate, milky, soft cheese, often used in Indian dishes. It can also be cut into cubes or crumbled over salads, pizzas or tagines, or used as part of a filling in savory phyllo or puff pastry bundles. Store-bought paneer tends to have a firmer texture and is good stir-fried until golden.

Homemade Paneer

Makes: *1 pound*   **Preparation time:** *10 minutes, plus 1 hour draining and 1 hour pressing*   **Cooking time:** *10 minutes*

4 cups whole milk
2 to 3 tablespoons lemon juice
1 teaspoon fine sea salt

1. Line a colander or strainer with a double layer of clean muslin or cheesecloth. Pour the milk into a pan and bring to a boil, then turn the heat down to low. Add 2 tablespoons of the lemon juice and stir until the milk separates into curds and whey. If the milk takes longer than a minute to curdle, add the remaining lemon juice to help get it going.

2. Remove the pan from the heat and pour the mixture into the lined colander. Rinse the curds briefly under cold running water to remove any sour residue from the lemon and stir in the salt. Draw up the corners of the muslin, twist to make a bundle and squeeze gently to remove as much liquid as possible. Press into a round disc and let the curds drain in the colander over a large mixing bowl, 1 hour.

3. When fully drained, put the muslin-covered curd bundle on a plate and press under a heavy weight. Put it in the refrigerator and leave 1 hour. Once the cheese is pressed, you can leave it whole or cut into cubes and store in a container covered with lightly salted water up to 4 days.

The lemon juice is added to encourage the heated milk to form curds, but the same quantity of buttermilk or thick plain yogurt will do the same job as the lemon juice.

Roasting intensifies the flavor of nuts (and seeds) as well as giving them more of a crunch. You get a more even roasting and color if this is done in the oven, rather than in a dry skillet, but if you only need a small quantity, then pan-toasting makes more sense. If I happen to be using the oven, I make the most of the space and heat by toasting the nuts in bulk; they'll keep fresh a week or so in an airtight container.

Roasted Nuts (and Seeds)

Makes: *2–4 handfuls*   **Preparation time:** *5 minutes*
Cooking time: *15 minutes*

2–4 handfuls of shelled nuts (or seeds) of choice

1. Preheat the oven to 350°F. Line one or two cookie sheets with parchment paper and put the nuts (or seeds) in an even layer on top. Put the cookie sheet(s) in the bottom half of the oven and roast 12 to 15 minutes (6 to 10 minutes for seeds), turning twice, until toasted and evenly browned. Keep an eye on them as they can burn easily. Alternatively, for small quantities of nuts (or seeds), put them in a dry, heavy-based frying pan in an even layer. Toast over a medium-low heat 8–10 minutes (5–7 minutes for seeds; 2–3 minutes for small seeds such as sesame), regularly shaking the pan, until toasted and evenly browned. Let cool and store in an airtight container.

If you regularly eat nuts and seeds it pays to buy them in large quantities. If packed in a plastic bag, transfer them after opening to an airtight container and store in a cool place—even the fridge or freezer—to keep them fresh. You don't have to defrost nuts and seeds before use.

A spoonful of this lightly spiced fresh mango chutney perks up curries, but is equally good served with cheese and crusty bread. Peaches, nectarines or pineapple would work as well as the mango, so feel free to adapt depending on what fruit you have available.

Mango Chutney

Makes: *1¼ cups*   **Preparation time:** *10 minutes*
Cooking time: *30 minutes*

1 tablespoon coriander seeds
1 tablespoon sunflower oil
1 small onion, finely chopped
1 green chili, finely chopped (no need to
   seed it)
1½-inch piece of ginger root, peeled and very
   finely chopped

8 cloves
1 large ripe mango, pitted and cubed
¼ cup white wine vinegar
¼ cup light brown sugar
sea salt and freshly ground black pepper

1. Toast the coriander seeds in a large, dry skillet over medium-low heat 2 minutes, or until aromatic. Lightly crush with a mortar and pestle or the end of a rolling pin. Set to one side.

2. Heat the oil in the skillet over medium heat. Add the onion and fry 7 minutes until tender but not colored. Stir in the chili, ginger and cloves, then add the mango, ¼ cup water, the vinegar and sugar, and stir well, and simmer 20 minutes until reduced and thickened. Season with salt and pepper, then taste, adding more sugar or vinegar as needed.

3. Spoon the chutney into sterilized jars (see page 11) or into a bowl and let cool. The chutney can be eaten right away but its flavor will develop with time. It will keep up to 2 weeks in the refrigerator.

This popular, spicy Korean pickled relish is the classic accompaniment to the rice dish Bibimbap (see page 75), but a spoonful will lift any Asian rice or noodle dish. The Asian radish, daikon or mooli is traditional but I find turnip is just as good, easier to find and more economical to buy.

Kimchi

Makes: *3 cups*   **Preparation time:** *2½ days*

¾ cup salt, plus extra for sprinkling
1 pound, 10 ounces Chinese cabbage, cut in
    half crosswise and cut into 4 wedges,
    tough stalk removed
13 ounces turnip, peeled and coarsely grated
3 tablespoons dark soy sauce
2 teaspoons mild Korean red pepper powder,
    Aleppo red pepper flakes or mild
    cayenne pepper

2 tablespoons gochujang (Korean hot chili
    paste) or other hot chili paste
1-inch piece of ginger root, grated
    (no need to peel)
2 garlic cloves, finely chopped
1 tablespoon sugar
1 tablespoon sesame seeds, toasted
4 scallions, sliced
1 teaspoon sesame oil

1. Dissolve the salt in 8 cups water in a large bowl. Sprinkle extra salt between the leaves of the cabbage. Put the cabbage in the salty water and put a weighted plate on top to keep it submerged. Let soak 3 hours, or until the cabbage leaves are pliable and do not break when bent.

2. Using a slotted spoon, scoop the cabbage out of the water into a large colander and add the grated turnip to the salted water. Rinse the cabbage well under cold running water (this is important or it will be too salty) and let drain 30 minutes while the turnip is soaking.

3. Mix together the soy sauce, red pepper powder, chili paste, ginger, garlic, sugar, sesame seeds, scallions and sesame oil in a large bowl.

4. Squeeze the cabbage to remove any excess water and pat dry with a clean dish towel. Slice the cabbage crosswise into large, bite-size pieces and add to the bowl with the flavorings. Drain and rinse the turnip well, drain again and pat dry in a clean dish towel. Add to the bowl with the cabbage and stir until everything is combined. Spoon the kimchi into a sterilized Mason jar (see page 11) and press down with the back of the spoon. Put the lid on and leave in a cool, dark place 2 days before eating, to allow the flavors to develop, then transfer to a refrigerator. It will keep several months in the refrigerator.

A piquant, fruity salsa that is good as a topping for bruschetta, served with roasted or barbecued vegetables, or as an accompaniment to the Goat Cheese Pancakes (see page 138).

Pomegranate Salsa

Serves: 4   Preparation time: 15 minutes   Cooking time: 35 minutes

1 tablespoon olive oil
1 onion, finely chopped
5 garlic cloves, finely chopped
2/3 cup white wine vinegar
2/3 cup fresh orange juice
3¼ tablespoons light brown sugar

seeds from 1 small pomegranate
2 handfuls pistachios, toasted
  (see page 18) and chopped
1 ounce mint leaves, roughly chopped
  (about 1 cup)
sea salt and freshly ground black pepper

1. Heat the oil in a saucepan over medium heat. Add the onion and fry 10 minutes until softened and starting to color, then add the garlic and cook another 2 minutes. Stir in the vinegar, orange juice and sugar, then turn the heat down to low and simmer 25 minutes, stirring occasionally, until the liquid has reduced and become syrupy. Season well with salt and pepper.

2. Transfer to a bowl and let cool slightly before stirring in the pomegranate seeds, pistachios and mint.

Middle Eastern markets are great places to buy large bunches of fresh herbs at a fraction of the cost of those sold in supermarkets. To keep them fresh a week or more, wrap the root end in a damp piece of paper towel, secure with an elastic band and store in a plastic bag. Alternatively remove the leaves from the stems and freeze them separately in plastic containers for future use.

This salsa crops up a fair bit in this book—I find it a great and easy way to add flavor, texture and interest to all sorts of dishes.

Tomato and Chili Salsa

Serves: 4   Preparation time: 15 minutes

4 large vine-ripened tomatoes, seeded
   and cubed
¼ red onion, chopped
2 heaped tablespoons bottled jalapeño
   chilies, drained and chopped

2 handfuls of cilantro, chopped
juice of 1 lime
2 tablespoons extra virgin olive oil
sea salt and freshly ground black pepper

1. Mix together all the ingredients for the salsa in a bowl. Season with salt and pepper and serve at room temperature.

This garlicky sweet potato and coconut milk mash is served with the Eggs with Lemongrass Cream (see page 125), but could be served topped with strips of omelet, marinated fried tofu or roasted vegetables.

Asian-Style Mash

Serves: 4   Preparation time: 15 minutes   Cooking time: 15 minutes

15 ounces sweet potatoes, peeled and cut into
   large pieces
15 ounces white potatoes, peeled and cut into
   large pieces
3 scallions, chopped

4 garlic cloves
scant ½ cup coconut milk
juice of ½ lime
1 medium red chili, seeded and
   finely chopped

1. Put both types of potato, the scallions (reserving a third of the green parts to serve) and garlic in a large saucepan, cover with just-boiled water from a kettle or from another pan and return to a boil. Turn the heat down slightly and simmer, part-covered, 10 to 15 minutes, or until tender. Drain and return the potatoes to the pan and let them dry briefly in the heat of the pan.

2. Add the coconut milk, lime juice and chili to the pan, season with salt and pepper and mash until smooth. Serve immediately.

A sprinkling of crisp, golden onions and ginger adds the finishing touch to Asian stir-fries, curries and salads. In fact, why be restricted to Asian food? I'd be tempted to add a spoonful to whatever you feel would benefit. It makes sense to cook up a large batch and then store any leftovers in an airtight container, lined with paper towels, in the refrigerator.

Crispy Onions and Ginger

Serves: 6–8   *Preparation time:* 10 minutes   *Cooking time:* 11 minutes

1 cup sunflower oil
2 onions, cut in half and thinly sliced into half-moons

4-inch piece of ginger root, peeled and cut into thin julienne strips

1. Heat the oil in a deep, heavy pan over medium heat. Add the onions and fry 6 to 8 minutes or until golden and crisp. They will crisp up more as they cool. Remove with a slotted spoon and drain on a double layer of paper towels.

2. Add the ginger to the pan and fry 3 minutes, or until golden and crisp. Drain the ginger and combine with the cooked onions. Let cool before using.

Store-bought preserved lemons can be fiendishly expensive, so not wishing to splash out or be left with a half-used jar in the refrigerator, I was eager to try a friend's speedy alternative—and the results were so good. Usually preserved lemons take months to preserve, but these take a matter of minutes and you still get that wonderful salty, lemony tang, which characterizes the traditionally made preserved lemons.

Quick Preserved Lemons

Makes: *about 1 cup*   **Preparation time:** *10 minutes, plus cooling*
Cooking time: *15 minutes*

6 unwaxed lemons
1½ teaspoons sea salt

1. Use a vegetable peeler to pare off the skin of each lemon, then cut in half and squeeze the juice and remove any seeds. Put the lemon skin and juice and salt into a non-reactive, small saucepan and slowly bring to boiling heat. Turn the heat down and simmer 10 to 12 minutes until the lemon skins are tender and the juice has reduced.

2. Transfer to a bowl and let cool. Use the preserved lemons right away or spoon into an airtight container and store in the refrigerator up to 2 weeks.

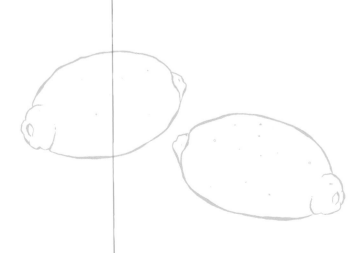

Elderflowers have a relatively short life so it makes sense to grab the opportunity to use them in cooking. A spoonful of this light and delicately fragrant syrup adds a touch of sweetness to marinades or dressings, or it can be used to flavor the poaching liquid for pears (see page 132) or other orchard fruit. Diluted with sparkling water or club soda, it makes a refreshing, summery drink.

Elderflower Syrup

Makes: *4 cups*   **Preparation time:** *15 minutes, plus 3 days infusing*
Cooking time: *10 minutes*

23 large elderflower heads
juice and finely grated zest of 5 lemons
5 cups sugar

1. Shake the elderflower heads to remove any dirt or bugs, then strip the flowers off the stalks and put them in a large heatproof bowl with the lemon juice and zest.

2. Meanwhile, bring 4 cups water to a boil in a pan. Stir in the sugar until dissolved, then boil 6 to 8 minutes until you have a light syrup.

3. Pour the syrup over the flower mixture, stir well, then cover and let infuse 3 days. Strain the flowers through a fine mesh strainer and pour the syrup into sterilized bottles (see page 11). The syrup will keep in the refrigerator up to 1 month.

Chapter 1
Can of Beans
(and Other Legumes)

You can't get a more humble food than a bean, yet the recipes here show that it's perfectly possible to create truly delicious meals with something so simple and unassuming: there's spicy Black Bean Tostadas with tangy Lime Cream, a filling Lentil, Preserved Lemon and Date Tagine, and a quick-to-make Edamame and Wasabi Hummus, and that's just a taster ... All recipes give instructions for using canned or dried beans, allowing you to make the most of what you have at hand.

Small bags of Chinese fermented black beans can be bought from Asian markets, and any leftovers will keep for months in an airtight container in the refrigerator. They're inexpensive, and pack a powerful punch. You could add cooked noodles or rice to this soup for a more substantial meal.

Oriental Black Bean and Mushroom Broth

Serves: 4   **Preparation time:** 15 minutes, plus making the stock and 30 minutes soaking and infusing   **Cooking time:** 10 minutes

4 cups Vegetable Stock (see page 14)

2 star anise

1-inch piece of ginger root, peeled and cut into round slices

2 tablespoons soy sauce

2 garlic cloves, cut in half

¼ cup Chinese fermented black beans

7 ounces shiitake or crimini mushrooms, thinly sliced

1 long red chili, seeded and thinly sliced

2 large handfuls of baby spinach leaves

1 heaped cup sugar snap peas, sliced diagonally

TO SERVE

2 teaspoons toasted sesame oil

2 eggs, lightly beaten

1 small handful of bean sprouts

2 scallions, thinly sliced on the diagonal

1 tablespoon roasted unsalted peanuts

1. Put the stock in a large pan and add the star anise, ginger, soy sauce and garlic. Bring to a boil over medium heat, then turn the heat off and let infuse 30 minutes, covered with a lid. Remove the flavorings with a slotted spoon.

2. Meanwhile, put the black beans in a small bowl, cover with 1 cup just-boiled water and let soak 30 minutes. Strain the beans, reserving the soaking liquor for another recipe (see below), and add the beans to the flavored stock along with the mushrooms and half the chili. Bring to a boil, then turn the heat down and simmer 1 minute. Add the spinach and sugar snaps, stir and simmer another 3 minutes until tender.

3. While the broth is simmering, make an omelet. Heat the sesame oil in a large, nonstick skillet, pour in the eggs, swirl the pan so they cover the bottom and cook 2 minutes until set. Roll up the omelet with a spatula, tip it onto a cutting board and cut crosswise into thin strips. Ladle the soup into four wide bowls and top with the omelet strips, beansprouts, remaining chili, scallions and chopped peanuts.

Freeze the soaking liquor from the fermented black beans in an ice cube tray. Transfer the cubes to a ziploc bag and return to the freezer. Use as a flavorsome stock.

Chinese black beans are also used in Chinese Black Bean and Mozzarella Salad (page 151).

To **sprout your own beans or seeds**, soak them in tepid water 12 hours, then drain and put in a clean jam jar. Cover with cheesecloth and secure with a rubber band, then stand in a light, draft-free place. Rinse twice a day under cold water (don't remove the cheesecloth), then drain. The sprouts are ready when they're 1 inch long. Store in an airtight container in the refrigerator up to 1 week.

Dandelions

grow profusely and you can forage for them at any time of the year, although I always pick the *young spring leaves* because they are less bitter. Choose a spot where they grow that is free from any kind of contamination—traffic and dogs, for example—and pick the leaves from the bottom of the plant. Trim the leaves and wash them well before using.

In southern Italy's Puglia region, this fava bean (dried broad bean) puree is a winter staple and a popular antipasto. Made from basic seasonal ingredients, it is pure comfort food when spread over crusty bread and doubles up as a satisfying side dish. The Pugliese serve it with bitter greens such as wild chicory, but you could use spinach, arugula, sea beet, nettles or broccoli rabe. I've gone for a mixture of young dandelion and beet leaves.

Fava Bean Puree

Serves: *4–6*   **Preparation time:** *15 minutes, plus overnight soaking*
Cooking time: *1 hour*

1 cup split dried fava beans, soaked overnight, drained and rinsed
10½ ounces white potatoes, peeled and thickly sliced
2 cups young dandelion leaves, roughly chopped
3 cups beet greens, tough stalks removed, leaves shredded
juice of ½ lemon

⅔ cup extra virgin olive oil, plus extra for drizzling
sea salt and freshly ground black pepper

TO SERVE
4 to 8 thick slices of country-style bread
2 garlic cloves, cut in half
4 vines of ripened cherry tomatoes

1. Tip the soaked fava beans into a large pot, cover with plenty of cold water and bring to a boil, then turn the heat down slightly and boil gently 40 minutes until tender. Drain the beans and return to the pot along with the potatoes. Cover with water and bring to a boil, then turn the heat down and simmer 20 minutes, or until the potatoes and beans are soft.

2. Meanwhile, put the dandelion leaves and beet leaves in a pot with a splash of water. Add a good pinch of salt to the pot and cook, covered, over low heat 3 minutes until softened. Stir the leaves occasionally so they cook evenly. Drain away any bitter juices, add another splash of water and cook, uncovered, another 2 minutes, or until the leaves are very tender and the water has evaporated. Drain off any excess water and set to one side.

3. Drain the fava beans and potatoes, reserving the cooking water, and return the beans and potatoes to the pot. Season well with salt and pepper and mash with a potato masher, adding the lemon juice and some of the reserved cooking water to make a thick, smooth, fluffy puree. Beat in the olive oil until combined. Transfer to a bowl and drizzle with oil. Toast the bread and rub one side of each slice with the cut side of a garlic clove. Serve the bean puree warm, topped with the greens and extra oil, with the garlic toasts and tomatoes.

Any leftover puree can be mixed with a beaten egg and formed into patties. Dust them in flour and fry in sunflower oil until crisp and golden.

A bag of frozen edamame (soy) beans makes a useful freezer standby for adding to stir-fries, soups or salads, or pureed—as here—to make a dip. Instead of adding wasabi, you can alter the flavorings to make a Moroccan-style hummus by adding extra tahini, ground coriander and cumin, and a little harissa. In keeping with the Asian feel, the hummus comes with wonton crisps.

Edamame and Wasabi Hummus

Serves: 4–6   **Preparation time:** 10 minutes, plus cooling
Cooking time: 5 minutes

1 heaped cup frozen edamame
   (soy) beans
2 teaspoons wasabi paste
juice of 1½ unwaxed limes
2 tablespoons light olive oil, plus extra
   for frying

1 tablespoon light tahini
1 tablespoon fresh chopped chives
1 tablespoon sesame seeds, toasted
   (see page 18), plus extra for sprinkling
sea salt and freshly ground black pepper
8 to 12 wonton wrappers for frying, to serve

1. Cook the edamame in a pan of boiling salted water 5 minutes until tender, then let cool in their cooking water. Drain the beans, reserving 4 to 6 tablespoons of the cooking water.

2. Put the cooled beans, reserving a handful, in a blender with the wasabi, lime juice, olive oil, tahini and reserved water, and blend to a coarse paste. Spoon the hummus into a serving bowl and season with salt and pepper. Serve at room temperature topped with the reserved beans, chives and sesame seeds.

3. To make the wonton crisps, pour in enough oil to coat the bottom of a large skillet and heat over medium heat. Fry the wontons in batches 1 to 2 minutes each side until crisp and golden. Drain on paper towels and, while still warm, season with salt and pepper and scatter sesame seeds on top.

Use the hummus as the filling for Wonton Ravioli (see page 59).

Finely grate the zest of the limes before you extract the juice, and store the zest in a small airtight container in the freezer up to 3 months. Use right from frozen whenever a recipe calls for lime zest. Orange and lemon zest can be frozen and used in the same way, too.

If you haven't tried squash seeds, you'll find they're too good to throw away, and are reminiscent of pumpkin seeds. Roast them to scatter over this North African-inspired salad, or eat as a snack sprinkled with soy sauce.

French Lentil, Squash and Chickpea Salad

Serves: 4   *Preparation time:* 20 minutes   *Cooking time:* 50 minutes

6 tablespoons extra virgin olive oil

3 heaped teaspoons harissa

1 small butternut squash, peeled, seeds reserved, cut into bite-size cubes

2 red onions, each cut into 8 wedges

1 cup drained canned chickpeas or cooked dried chickpeas (see pages 8–9)

1⅓ cups dried French lentils

½ teaspoon cumin seeds

1 handful of parsley leaves, chopped

1 handful of cilantro, chopped

juice and finely grated zest of 1 large unwaxed lemon

4½ ounces rindless goat cheese, crumbled

sea salt and freshly ground black pepper

1. Preheat the oven to 400°F. Mix together 2 tablespoons of the oil and half the harissa in a large bowl. Season with salt and pepper and add the squash and onions, turn to coat them in the harissa oil, then tip into a large roasting pan and spread out in a single layer.

2. Wash the squash seeds, then add to the bowl along with the chickpeas. Pour in 1 tablespoon of the oil and the remaining harissa, turn until coated and tip out into a second large roasting pan. Spread them out in a single layer. Put both trays in the oven and roast 35 to 40 minutes, turning once, until the squash and onions are tender and slightly golden and the chickpeas and seeds are crisp.

3. Meanwhile, put the lentils in a saucepan, cover with plenty of cold water and bring to a boil. Turn the heat down to medium-low, part-cover with a lid and simmer 25 minutes until tender. Drain and tip into a serving bowl. Add the roasted squash, onions, cumin and herbs to the lentils. Mix together the remaining oil and lemon juice and zest, season with salt and pepper and pour it over the salad. Toss, then sprinkle with the goat cheese, chickpeas and 2 tablespoons of the squash seeds. The remaining squash seeds can be eaten separately as a snack.

Save time by cooking dried chickpeas in bulk (see pages 8–9), and store unused cooked chickpeas in the refrigerator up to 3 days or freeze up to 3 months. There's no need to defrost them for soups, stews or sauces.

Many of my recipes come about through a need to use up a motley collection of ingredients in the refrigerator or cupboard, and this is one of them. A package of dried green lentils and some ready-to-eat dried dates had been lurking in the cupboard and were crying out to be used. I also picked up a recipe for super-quick preserved lemons from a friend and was eager to put it to use. Jars of preserved lemons are prohibitively expensive and this version is a fantastically easy and economical alternative.

Lentil, Preserved Lemon and Date Tagine

Serves: *4–6*   **Preparation time:** *20 minutes, plus making the stock*
Cooking time: *35 minutes*

1 tablespoon olive oil
1 large onion, chopped
3 carrots, cut in half lengthwise and cut into
    bite-size chunks
2 turnips, peeled and cut into bite-size chunks
3 garlic cloves, chopped
2 teaspoons coriander seeds
2 cinnamon sticks
2 teaspoons ground cumin
1 teaspoon turmeric powder
½ teaspoon ground ginger

½ teaspoon dried red pepper flakes
heaped ¾ cup dried green lentils
3⅔ cups hot Vegetable Stock (see page 14)
⅔ cup ready-to-eat pitted dried dates,
    cut in half
1 tablespoon Quick Preserved Lemons
    (see page 24)
sea salt and freshly ground black pepper
1 handful of cilantro leaves, chopped,
    and couscous, to serve

1. Heat the olive oil in a large heavy pan over medium heat. Add the onion and cook 5 minutes until softened. Turn the heat down slightly and add the carrots, turnips, garlic and coriander seeds and cook, part-covered, another 5 minutes, stirring regularly, until the carrots have softened slightly.

2. Stir in the cinnamon sticks, ground spices and red pepper flakes, then add the lentils. Pour in the stock, stir well and bring to a boil. Turn the heat down to low, part-cover the pan with a lid and simmer 15 minutes until the lentils are almost tender.

3. Stir in the dates and the preserved lemons and cook, covered, 10 minutes, or until the lentils are tender. Add a splash more stock or water, if the tagine needs it. Season with salt and pepper, scatter the cilantro over it and serve in bowls with couscous on the side.

Why buy a can of refried beans when you can make your own for less, and they taste a whole lot better? Packs of four small avocados may be more economical than individual ones, and are just the right size for salads.

Black Bean Tostadas with Lime Cream

Serves: 4   *Preparation time:* 15 minutes   *Cooking time:* 10 minutes

2½ cups drained canned black beans, liquid reserved, or cooked dried black beans (see pages 8–9), reserving ¼ cup of the cooking water
½ red onion, cut in half
1 large garlic clove
juice of ½ lime
2 tablespoons olive oil
2 teaspoons chipotle chili paste
1 teaspoon ground cumin
1 teaspoon ground coriander

4 soft corn tortillas
½ Romaine lettuce, shredded
2 small avocados, pitted, peeled and sliced
1 cup feta cheese, crumbled
sea salt and freshly ground black pepper
1 recipe quantity Tomato and Chili Salsa (see page 22), to serve

LIME CREAM
scant ½ cup crème fraîche or sour cream
finely grated zest of ½ unwaxed lime

1. Mix together the ingredients for the lime cream in a bowl, cover and leave in the refrigerator until needed.

2. Put half the black beans along with the onion, garlic, lime juice and ¼ cup of the drained liquid from the beans in a blender. Pulse briefly to a coarse puree, then tip into a medium, nonstick skillet with 1 tablespoon of the oil, the remaining beans, chipotle chili paste, cumin and coriander. Season with salt and pepper, stir and cook over medium-low heat 5 minutes until heated through.

3. Meanwhile, heat the remaining oil in a separate skillet and cook the tortillas, one at a time, 1 minute on each side until heated through and golden in places. Put a tortilla on each serving plate and top with the lettuce, refried beans, avocados and feta. Serve with the salsa and lime cream.

A tip for cooking dried beans is to add a 5-inch strip of kombu (dried kelp used in Japanese cooking) to the cooking liquid. This helps soften the outer skin and gives a creamier, softer texture. The kombu works by breaking down the starchy carbohydrates in the beans.

If you have memories of soggy, mealy lima beans served up in your childhood, ditch that thought now and try them in this light, summery stew. One of my favorite spices is hot smoked paprika—it not only satisfies my love of chili-heat, but its wonderful smokiness brings a dish together.

Spanish-Style White Beans

Serves: 4   **Preparation time:** 15 minutes, plus making the stock
Cooking time: 45 minutes

3 tablespoons extra virgin olive oil
1 large onion, chopped
3 large garlic cloves, thinly sliced
1 large red bell pepper, seeded and chopped
2 zucchini, sliced, and each slice quartered
2/3 cup dry white wine or extra vegetable
  stock (see below)
2 cups tomato puree
2/3 cup Vegetable Stock
  (see page 14)
1 teaspoon sugar

2½ cups drained canned lima beans, or
  cooked dried lima beans (see pages 8–9)
2 bay leaves
1 tablespoon thyme leaves or 2 teaspoons
  dried thyme
1 to 2 teaspoons hot smoked paprika
3 handfuls of curly kale or cavalo nero
  (black kale), tough stalks removed,
  leaves shredded
sea salt and freshly ground black pepper
sour cream and crusty bread, to serve

1. Heat the olive oil in a large heavy pan over medium heat. Add the onion and fry 6 minutes until softened. Add the garlic, red bell pepper and zucchini and cook another 5 minutes until just tender.

2. Pour in the wine and bring to a boil. Cook until reduced by half, then add the tomato puree and vegetable stock and return to a boil. Turn the heat down to low, add the sugar, lima beans, bay leaves, thyme and paprika, and simmer, part-covered, 30 minutes until the sauce has thickened.

3. Stir in the kale, season with salt and pepper and cook another 3 minutes until wilted. Serve with crusty bread, and topped with a spoonful of sour cream.

Save time and freezer space by freezing stews, soups, sauces and curries flat. Once they've cooled, transfer to a ziploc bag and put on a cookie sheet in the freezer. To defrost, hold under a hot faucet a few seconds, then unzip the bag and tip the contents into a pan to reheat.

In a small garden, grow *zucchini* in pots. The seeds should be sown indoors in mid-spring, and the young plants planted out when there is no risk of frost. Female stems have a small bulge behind the flower that will turn into a zucchini; males just produce flowers. Don't waste the flowers—harvest them early in the day, remove the stamens and stuff with ricotta, then fry in a light tempura batter.

☞ Tofu

isn't to everyone's taste, but if you treat it as a blank canvas and are brave with your flavorings and textures, it can be transformed into something quite special. It's important to drain tofu well and pat it dry using paper towels, as you don't want any residual water to dilute your marinade or soften a golden crust. Use a feisty marinade, a thick sticky glaze, or coat in cornstarch, batter or breadcrumbs to give a crisp crust. I like the way tofu readily takes on other flavors and can be adapted to suit different styles of cooking: it's perfect in Asian dishes, but also works in Western tomato-based dishes and hearty broths. Look out for smoked tofu (with sesame seeds is particularly good); silken tofu, which can be blended to make creamy sauces; and golden fried tofu that needs very little embellishment.

▶▶

Slices of rosemary- and garlic-marinated tofu are coated in breadcrumbs and fried until crisp and golden, then served with a punchy salsa. Any slightly stale bread (including crusts) can be turned into breadcrumbs, and I like to keep a ready supply in the freezer.

Tofu Cutlets with Salsa

Serves: *4*　**Preparation time:** *20 minutes, plus 1 hour marinating*
Cooking time: *12 minutes*

1 pound firm tofu, drained, patted dry and
　　sliced into 8 approximately ½-inch slices
2 eggs
1¼ cups day-old breadcrumbs or Japanese
　　panko crumbs
finely grated zest of 1 large unwaxed lemon
⅓ cup sunflower oil
sea salt and freshly ground black pepper

MARINADE
2 tablespoons extra virgin olive oil
2 large garlic cloves, crushed
1 heaped tablespoon finely chopped
　　rosemary leaves

TO SERVE
¾ cup drained canned flageolet beans,
　　or cooked dried flageolet beans
　　(see pages 8–9)
1 recipe quantity Tomato and Chili Salsa
　　(see page 22)
juice of 1 large unwaxed lemon
arugula salad

1. Mix together the ingredients for the marinade and season well with salt and pepper. Put the tofu in a large, shallow dish, spoon the marinade over it and spread it over both sides. Let it marinate, covered, 1 hour.

2. Meanwhile, mix the flageolet beans into the salsa, using the lemon juice instead of lime.

3. Beat the eggs in a shallow dish. Put the breadcrumbs and lemon zest in a separate shallow dish and season with salt and pepper. Heat the sunflower oil in a large skillet over medium heat. Dip the tofu slices into the egg and then the crumbs until coated all over, then fry 3 minutes on each side until golden (in two batches if necessary). Drain on paper towels and serve with the salsa and an arugula salad.

Pictured on page 41.

▶▶ Smoked Tofu and Mango Salad

To make this zingy Asian-inspired salad, start with the dressing. Mix together **⅓ cup light olive oil**, **the juice of 1 lime** and **2 teaspoons peeled and finely chopped ginger root** and season with **salt** and **pepper**. Put **2 handfuls of arugula leaves** and **half a roughly chopped romaine lettuce** on a serving plate, then scatter over it **½ chopped red onion**, **6 thinly sliced radishes**, **1 seeded and finely chopped medium red chili** and **1 peeled mango, cubed**. Heat **1 tablespoon light olive oil** in a large skillet and fry **3 cups cubed smoked tofu** 3 minutes, turning once, until golden. Pour the dressing over the salad and toss until combined, then scatter over it the smoked tofu and a **small handful of torn cilantro** and **chopped chives**.

▶▶ Crispy Thai-Spiced Tofu

Mix together **3 tablespoons cornstarch**, **1 tablespoon Thai 7-spice**, **1 teaspoon smoked mild paprika** and **salt** and **pepper** in a large, flat dish. Dunk **1 pound tofu** cut into 8 approximately ½-inch slices into the cornstarch mixture until coated all over. Heat **⅔ cup sunflower oil** in a large, nonstick skillet over medium heat. Fry the tofu 3 to 4 minutes each side until golden and crisp. Drain on paper towels. Serve sprinkled with **2 chopped scallions**, **2 tablespoons chopped cilantro** and **1 long red seeded and chopped chili**.

▶▶ Tofu Bahn Mi

To make this Franco-Vietnamese baguette, mix together **3 tablespoons rice vinegar** and **2 teaspoons honey** in a bowl and stir in **1 grated carrot** and a **2-inch piece of seeded and shredded cucumber**. Mix together **2 teaspoons hot chili sauce** and **2 tablespoons soy sauce** in a dish. Add **10 to 14 ounces tofu**, cut into 4 approximately ⅝-inch slices. Season with **salt** and **pepper** and turn the tofu in the marinade. Let the vegetables and tofu marinate at least 30 minutes. Fry the tofu in **¼ cup sunflower oil** 6 minutes, turning once, until crisp on both sides. Spread **4 small baguettes** with **mayonnaise** and top with **lettuce**, the drained carrot and cucumber mixture, the fried tofu, a **few cilantro leaves** and an **extra splash of chili sauce**, if you like.

Chapter 2
Pack of Pasta
(and Noodles)

So simple, so versatile, so economical: a pack of pasta is the perfect foundation for many meat-free meals. In this chapter, it's at the heart of the Linguine Carbonara with Crispy Capers, Fettuccine with Asparagus and Wild Garlic Pesto, and Creamy Porcini and Sea Beet Orzo. Let's not forget noodles, either, which are equally diverse. For starters, there's Wonton Ravioli with Arugula, Pho with Kale Chips, and Burmese Noodle, Tofu and Winter Greens Curry. All completely different dishes, yet with a common theme.

This Provençal soup, known as pistou, is great for using up boxes of pasta lurking in the cupboard that don't quite hold enough for a whole meal but which you don't want to go to waste, either. Feel free to swap the veg, depending on what you have on hand, and the basil sauce can be made with a mixture of herbs, including oregano, thyme, marjoram and arugula.

Provençal Soup

Serves: 4   **Preparation time:** 15 minutes, plus making the stock
Cooking time: 20 minutes

1 heaped tablespoon butter
2 leeks, sliced
2 carrots, chopped
1 celery stalk, sliced
1 fennel bulb, sliced
1 bouquet garni, made up of a large bay leaf
   and a few thyme and parsley sprigs
4 cups Vegetable Stock (see page 14)
2½ ounces spaghettini or dried pasta shape
   of choice
scant 2 cups drained canned lima beans or
   cooked dried lima beans (see pages 8–9)

2 zucchini, quartered lengthwise and sliced
½ cup fresh shelled peas or frozen peas
4 thick slices of day-old country-style bread

BASIL SAUCE
4 large handfuls of basil leaves, plus extra
   to serve
2 garlic cloves
⅓ cup plus 2 teaspoons extra virgin olive oil
heaped ⅓ cup finely grated vegetarian
   parmesan cheese, plus extra to serve
sea salt and freshly ground black pepper

1. Melt the butter in a large, heavy pot over medium heat. Add the leeks, carrots, celery, fennel and bouquet garni and cook 10 minutes, stirring regularly, until softened.

2. Pour in the stock and bring to a boil. Add the pasta and gently boil 5 minutes until almost tender, then add the lima beans, zucchini and peas and cook another 5 minutes until tender.

3. Meanwhile, heat a ridged grill pan over high heat and grill the bread until toasted on both sides and blackened in places.

4. To make the basil sauce, put the basil, garlic and oil in a blender and blend until smooth. Transfer to a bowl, stir in the parmesan and season with salt and pepper. Taste, and add more parmesan, if you like. Put a slice of toasted bread in each serving bowl—a wide, shallow one is best—and ladle the soup over it, removing the bouquet garni first. Spoon the basil sauce on top and serve with extra parmesan and basil leaves.

Don't throw away the rind from hard cheeses such as parmesan, as they can be added to soups and stews to add an umami (savory) richness to the broth.

Carrots

thrive in fine, sandy soil. Sow the seeds thinly in shallow drills in spring. Water regularly and protect seedlings with a plastic bottle, open top and bottom. You'll be rewarded with crisp, sweet carrots in the summer. Late-sown seeds will be ready in early fall. The main enemy of the carrot is the carrot fly. Leeks, onions, rosemary and sage repel them, so sow these next to your row of carrots.

If you are new to culinary gardening, try *growing your own herbs*. Seeds are more economical; young plants are quicker to establish. Start with oregano, thyme, basil, chives, rosemary, sage, coriander, mint, bay leaves and flat-leaf parsley. Mint is best grown in a container; coriander and basil need a sheltered sunny spot. Hardy bay, rosemary and sage provide fresh herbs throughout the year.

The taste of this pasta dish belies the fact that it's made from humble, simple ingredients. Even the eggplant skin does not go to waste, as it's cut into thin strips, fried until crisp and piled on top of the pasta just before serving.

Spaghetti with Eggplant, Cheese and Mint

Serves: 4   *Preparation time:* 15 minutes   *Cooking time:* 25 minutes

2 eggplants
¼ cup extra virgin olive oil, plus extra
   for drizzling
14 ounces dried spaghetti
1 onion, finely chopped
1 garlic clove, finely chopped
4 tomatoes, seeded and chopped

1 tablespoon tomato paste
1 cup drained canned chickpeas or cooked
   dried chickpeas (see pages 8–9)
1 handful of mint leaves
sea salt and freshly ground black pepper
scant ½ cup mature vegetarian sheep cheese,
   grated, to serve

1. Using a vegetable peeler, remove the skin from the eggplants in strips. Cut the skin into thin strips and set aside. Cube the flesh. Heat the oil in a large, deep skillet over medium heat and fry the eggplant skins 2 to 3 minutes until crisp, then remove using a slotted spoon and drain on paper towels. Add the cubed eggplant to the pan and fry 8 minutes, or until light golden all over.

2. Meanwhile, bring a large pot of salted water to a boil and cook the spaghetti following the package instructions. Drain, reserving ⅓ cup of the cooking water.

3. Add the onion to the eggplant and cook another 8 minutes until softened, then add the garlic, tomatoes, tomato paste and chickpeas. Cook over medium-low heat 5 minutes, stirring often and adding enough of the reserved pasta cooking water to loosen the mixture and make a sauce.

4. Just before serving, stir in the mint and season with salt and pepper. Spoon the sauce on top of the pasta, drizzle with a little extra oil and serve with the fried eggplant skins and cheese piled on top.

Freeze tomato paste in teaspoon-sized piles on a baking sheet until solid. Transfer to a ziploc bag when frozen and return to the freezer to use as needed.

This is one of my favorite summer pasta dishes. It's light, quick, full of flavor and became a mainstay meal at home one summer as it admirably used up a glut of zucchini (see page 39). Walnut pieces are cheaper than halved or whole nuts, and are perfect for the dish, saving you preparation time.

Zucchini, Feta and Walnut Cavatappi

Serves: 4   *Preparation time:* 15 minutes   *Cooking time:* 15 minutes

14 ounces dried cavatappi or pasta shape
   of choice
¼ cup extra virgin olive oil
4 scallions, chopped, green and white parts
   kept separate
2 large garlic cloves, finely chopped
1 red chili, seeded and chopped
3 zucchini, coarsely grated

juice and finely grated zest of
   2 unwaxed lemons
1 cup feta cheese, cut into pieces
¾ cup walnut pieces,
   toasted (see page 18)
1 handful of basil or oregano leaves, torn
sea salt and freshly ground black pepper

1. Bring a large pot of salted water to a boil and cook the pasta following the package instructions. Drain, reserving ¼ cup of the cooking water, and return the pasta to the pot.

2. Meanwhile, heat the oil in a large skillet over medium-low heat. Add the white part of the scallions, the garlic and the chili, and fry 2 minutes until softened but not browned. Add the zucchini and lemon zest and cook another minute, then pour in the reserved pasta cooking water and lemon juice and heat through briefly.

3. Add the zucchini mixture to the cooked pasta. Season with salt and pepper and toss until combined. Serve with the green part of the scallions, the feta, the toasted walnuts and the herbs scattered over the top.

A handful of ingredients are transformed into a satisfying dish. Keep any spare chili oil for frying eggs, salad dressings or stirring into noodles. Store in a sterilized jar (see page 11) in a cool, dark place.

Rigatoni with Golden Lemon Crumbs

Serves: 4   **Preparation time:** 10 minutes, plus at least 30 minutes infusing
Cooking time: 15 minutes

14 ounces dried rigatoni
¾ cup day-old breadcrumbs
finely grated zest of 1 large unwaxed lemon
5 large handfuls of curly kale, tough stalks
   removed, leaves shredded
3 large garlic cloves, finely chopped
sea salt and freshly ground black pepper

2 tablespoons sunflower seeds, toasted
   (see page 18), to serve (optional)

CHILI OIL
½ cup extra virgin olive oil
8 to 10 small dried chilies (quantity will
   depend on their heat)

1. To make the chili oil, pour the oil into a small pan, add the chilies and heat gently 5 minutes. Remove from the heat and let infuse at least 30 minutes.

2. Bring a large pot of salted water to a boil and cook the pasta. Drain, reserving a scant ½ cup of the cooking water. Return the pasta and reserved cooking water to the pot.

3. Meanwhile, heat 1 tablespoon of the chili oil in a large, deep skillet over medium heat. Add the breadcrumbs and fry 4 minutes, turning them regularly, until light golden and crisp. Stir in the lemon zest and briefly heat through, then tip into a bowl.

4. Add 3 more tablespoons of chili oil to the skillet and heat over medium heat. Add the kale and stir-fry 3 to 4 minutes until tender. Add the garlic and cook 1 minute. Transfer the kale to the pot and toss. Season with salt and pepper and sprinkle with the lemon breadcrumbs and sunflower seeds, if using.

Instead of throwing away stale bread, blitz it—crusts and all—in a grinder or small food processor until you have coarse and/or fine crumbs. Store the breadcrumbs in an airtight container in the freezer up to 3 months, and use straight from frozen.

Capers aren't to everyone's taste—in fact I'm not a huge fan of them myself—but when fried until crisp they add a delicious piquant salty bite, in perfect contrast to the creaminess of the carbonara sauce. Do try this, as they really are something else when cooked in this way.

Linguine Carbonara with Crispy Capers

Serves: 4   *Preparation time:* 5 minutes   *Cooking time:* 15 minutes

14 ounces dried linguine

1 tablespoon olive oil

⅓ cup bottled capers, drained, rinsed and patted dry

3 tablespoons butter

3 vine-ripened tomatoes, seeded and chopped

2 large garlic cloves, finely chopped

1⅓ cups vegetarian parmesan cheese, grated

3 large eggs, lightly beaten

1 tablespoon chopped oregano leaves or 2 teaspoons dried oregano

sea salt and freshly ground black pepper

1. Bring a large pot of salted water to a boil and cook the pasta following the package instructions.

2. Meanwhile, heat the oil in a large, deep skillet over medium heat. Add the capers, turn the heat down slightly and fry 3 to 4 minutes, turning occasionally, until golden and crisp, then drain on paper towels. Add the butter to the pan and when melted, stir in the tomatoes and garlic and cook 3 minutes until softened, taking care that the garlic doesn't burn.

3. Mix three-quarters of the parmesan into the beaten eggs. When the pasta is cooked, use tongs to transfer it to the skillet and reserve the pasta cooking water. Take the skillet off the heat and quickly pour in the egg mixture. Using tongs, turn the linguine so it becomes evenly coated in the egg mixture, which should thicken without scrambling. Add 2 to 4 tablespoons of the pasta cooking water, if needed, to keep the pasta moist and to give a glossy sauce. Serve seasoned with pepper and sprinkled with the remaining parmesan and oregano.

Give tomatoes a good sniff before buying, and if they don't smell of tomatoes, skip it as they won't taste of anything either. Store tomatoes at room temperature—the cold of the refrigerator will affect their taste and texture, turning the flesh mealy and suppressing the flavor.

Homemade pesto takes a matter of minutes and is fresher and cheaper than store-bought, especially with foraged ingredients. Pesto can be so much more than the classic Ligurian basil version, and adapted to suit seasonal ingredients. Wild garlic leaves have just enough garlicky flavor without being too overpowering, and if you do manage to discover a sizeable patch, make a double batch of pesto and freeze it. Pine nuts can vary in quality, so try almonds, cashews, walnuts or Brazil nuts, for a sweet, nutty creaminess.

Fettuccine with Asparagus and Wild Garlic Pesto

Serves: 4   *Preparation time:* 10 minutes   *Cooking time:* 15 minutes

14 ounces dried fettuccine
5½ ounces asparagus tips, trimmed

WILD GARLIC PESTO
2 large handfuls of wild garlic leaves, flowers (if any) reserved (or use chive flowers)

1 handful of blanched almonds
⅓ cup plus 1 tablespoon mild-flavored extra virgin olive oil, plus extra for topping
1 handful of finely grated vegetarian parmesan cheese, plus extra to serve
sea salt and freshly ground black pepper

1. Bring a large pot of salted water to a boil and cook the pasta following the package instructions. Add the asparagus about 3 minutes before the pasta is ready. Drain, reserving ¼ cup of the pasta cooking water, and return the cooked pasta and asparagus to the pot.

2. Meanwhile, make the pesto. Put the wild garlic leaves and almonds in a mini food processor and blend until finely chopped. Continue to blend, adding the oil in two batches, and the parmesan, then season with salt and pepper. Spoon the pesto into a bowl or jar and drizzle some extra olive oil over the top. (It will keep up to 3 days in the refrigerator.)

3. Add as much pesto and reserved cooking water as needed to coat the pasta and asparagus, then turn the pasta until it is evenly coated. Taste and add extra salt and pepper, if needed. Serve sprinkled with more parmesan and wild garlic flowers, if you have them.

Use leftover cooked long pasta to make a frittata. Just stir the pasta into the egg mixture with a handful of grated Romano, and cook following the instructions on page 119.

Wild garlic makes an excellent alternative to garlic or chives in dishes, and is best left raw or lightly cooked. You can find wild garlic (you'll probably be able to smell it before you see it) with its broad, spear-like leaves in woody areas, hedge banks or waysides. The plant also has delicate white flowers on top of a thin stem— both leaves and flowers are edible.

I'd walked past small clumps of *sea beet leaves* on a local beach for years and never really considered that they could be edible. However, when I tried them I found that they had a *taste reminiscent of spinach*—but with none of that tartness you might expect. Make sure that you pick the young leaves, keep away from where dogs may have been and wash well before using.

OK, dried porcini may be pricey on the face of it, but a little goes a long way and the soaking water also turns into a wonderful, rich stock. Orzo is a small, rice-shaped pasta and makes a good alternative to grains. There's something very comforting and humble about orzo, which is also featured in the Scamorza, Orzo and Basil Oil Salad (see page 151)—it might be worth cooking up double the quantity. If you can't find sea beet (see opposite), you could use spinach, kale, cavolo nero or chard instead.

Creamy Porcini and Sea Beet Orzo

Serves: 4   *Preparation time:* 10 minutes, plus making the stock and 20 minutes soaking   *Cooking time:* 25 minutes

1 ounce dried porcini
3 tablespoons olive oil
10 ounces chestnut (or crimini) mushrooms, sliced
5½ ounces sea beet, spinach or chard, stalks thinly sliced and set aside, and leaves shredded (about 3 cups)

2 teaspoons thyme leaves or 1 teaspoon dried thyme
1½ cups Vegetable Stock (see page 14)
½ cup crème fraîche or sour cream
3 cups orzo pasta
sea salt and freshly ground black pepper
grated vegetarian parmesan cheese, to serve

1. Put the porcini in a bowl and cover with 1 cup just-boiled water. Let soak 20 minutes until softened. Strain the mushrooms, reserving the soaking liquid.

2. Heat the olive oil in a large, deep skillet over medium heat. Add the soaked porcini and fry 5 minutes until slightly crisp. Add the fresh mushrooms and continue to cook another 5 minutes, stirring regularly, until starting to color and turn crisp. The fresh mushrooms will appear dry at first and will then release liquid, which you want to cook out, otherwise they will be soggy. Stir in the sea beet stalks and thyme and cook another 2 minutes.

3. Pour in the stock and soaking liquid (leaving any gritty bits in the bottom of the bowl) and bring to a boil, then turn the heat down to low. Add the sea beet leaves and simmer 5 to 7 minutes until reduced by a third. Stir in the crème fraîche and simmer another 2 minutes until slightly reduced.

4. Meanwhile, cook the orzo in a large pot of boiling salted water following the package instructions. Drain, reserving ⅓ cup of the cooking water. Add the cooked orzo to the mushroom sauce with enough of the reserved pasta cooking water to make a fairly loose sauce, then turn until everything is mixed together. Season with salt and pepper and serve sprinkled with parmesan.

Another recipe using porcini is Rainbow Chard and Parmesan Tortino (see page 128).

Tahini, a thick paste made from ground sesame seeds, is traditionally used in hummus, but I like the nutty creaminess it gives the stock for this Japanese-inspired noodle dish. As a bonus, tahini is a valuable source of protein. Sprinkle the wild garlic flowers over the broth just before serving.

Udon Noodle Pot with Tahini and Wild Garlic

Serves: *4*   **Preparation time:** *20 minutes, plus making the stock*
Cooking time: *10 minutes*

¼ cup light soy sauce
2 teaspoons sugar
½ teaspoon dried red pepper flakes
1 tablespoon grated ginger root, peeled
2 heaped tablespoons light tahini
2½ cups Vegetable Stock (see page 14)
1 handful of wild garlic, leaves cut crosswise
   into strips, flowers reserved (if any)
2 tablespoons sunflower oil

1 large onion, sliced
10½ ounces mixed mushrooms, such as
   shiitake, crimini or oyster, sliced
2 bok choy, white parts thinly sliced and
   leaves thickly sliced
1 pound, 12 ounces soft udon noodles
sea salt and freshly ground black pepper
Crispy Onions and Ginger (see page 23),
   to serve (optional)

1. Mix together the soy sauce, sugar, red pepper flakes, ginger and tahini in a pan until combined. Pour in the stock and reserved noodle-cooking water and heat slowly until hot, stirring occasionally. (Do not overheat the tahini stock or it may curdle.) Stir in the wild garlic leaves and set to one side.

2. Heat the oil in a large wok and stir-fry the onion 3 minutes until softened slightly. Add the mushrooms and the white part of the bok choy and stir-fry another 5 minutes, then add the green part of the bok choy and stir-fry a final 2 minutes until the mushrooms are starting to crisp up and the leaves are tender but still crisp.

3. Meanwhile, bring a large pot of water to a boil and cook the noodles following the package instructions. Drain the noodles and divide into four large, shallow bowls. Ladle the stock over the noodles and top with the mushroom mixture. Sprinkle with the wild garlic flowers, if using, and Crispy Onions and Ginger, if you like.

For foraging wild garlic, see page 55.

Wonton wrappers are used as an alternative to pasta to make ravioli. And, continuing the fusion theme, the wonton skins are filled with Edamame and Wasabi Hummus (see page 32). Serve with a buttery ginger sauce.

Wonton Ravioli with Arugula

Serves: 4   **Preparation time:** *20 minutes, plus making the hummus*
Cooking time: *20 minutes*

40 square wonton wrappers for steaming
   (rather than frying)
¾ recipe quantity Edamame and Wasabi
   Hummus (see page 32)
1 to 2 teaspoons sea salt, to taste
1 cup (1 stick) minus 1 tablespoon butter
1½-inch piece of ginger root, peeled,
   finely grated and juice squeezed out

juice of ½ lime
1 handful of roughly chopped toasted walnuts
   (see page 18)
1 heaped tablespoon chopped chives
1 handful of arugula leaves
freshly ground black pepper

1. To make the ravioli, lay half the wonton wrappers on a large sheet of wax paper. Spoon a tablespoon of the hummus into the middle of each one and brush the edges of the wrappers with water. Top each one with a second wonton wrapper and press the edges together to seal. Turn the ravioli over so they are resting on their tops to prevent them sticking to the paper.

2. Fill a large pot with water, add the salt and bring to a boil. Cook the ravioli in four batches 3 to 5 minutes until the wontons are tender, keeping each batch warm on a large covered warm plate.

3. Meanwhile, to make the sauce, melt the butter in a pan. Add the ginger juice and cook over low heat 2 minutes to infuse, then season with salt and pepper. Spoon the ginger butter over the ravioli and serve with a squeeze of lime juice and scattered with the walnuts, chives and arugula.

Wonton wrappers can be found frozen or chilled in Asian stores and some supermarkets; there are those suited to steaming, while others need to be fried. I like to keep a pack in the freezer as they take little time to defrost and are great for making dumplings, crisps or, as here, ravioli.

For a bit of crunch, I've topped this Vietnamese noodle soup with kale chips, reminiscent of crispy seaweed and delicious sprinkled over rice or noodles, or enjoyed as a nutritious snack.

Pho with Kale Chips

Serves: 4   **Preparation time:** 15 minutes, plus making the stock
Cooking time: 20 minutes

1 recipe quantity Asian Stock (see page 15)
3½ baby spinach leaves
1 long red chili, seeded and thinly
   sliced diagonally
3 scallions, thinly sliced diagonally, white
   and green parts kept separate
1 teaspoon sesame oil
2 tablespoons light soy sauce
9 ounces thick dried rice noodles
2 carrots, cut into matchsticks
1 small red bell pepper, cut into thin strips

2 tablespoons roughly chopped cilantro
2 tablespoons roughly chopped mint leaves
sea salt and freshly ground black pepper
2 teaspoons sesame seeds, toasted, to serve

KALE CHIPS
1 tablespoon sesame oil
1 teaspoon light soy sauce
3 large handfuls of curly kale, larger stalks
   removed, leaves torn into large pieces
   if necessary

1. To make the kale chips, preheat the oven to 315°F. Mix together the sesame oil and soy sauce in a large bowl. Add the kale, and toss with your hands until coated. Scatter the kale over a large cookie sheet in an even layer. Bake 15 to 20 minutes, turning once or twice, until crisp but still green. Transfer the kale to a bowl and set one side.

2. Meanwhile, pour the Asian stock into a large pot and bring to a boil over medium heat, then let it bubble away 3 minutes. Strain and discard the flavorings, then return the stock to the pot and add the spinach, half the chili and the white part of the scallions. Turn the heat down slightly and simmer 3 minutes until the spinach has wilted.

3. Stir in the sesame oil and soy sauce and season with pepper (the stock should be salty enough, but you can add salt if you like) and heat through briefly.

4. Cook the rice noodles until tender, then drain and refresh under cold running water. Divide the noodles, carrots, red bell pepper, green part of the scallions, cilantro and mint into four large, shallow bowls. Ladle the stock over them, sprinkle with the sesame seeds and put a pile of the kale chips in the middle of each bowl.

Store fresh chilies, lemongrass, kaffir lime leaves and curry leaves in an airtight container or small ziploc bag in the freezer. There's no need to defrost before using.

Soba Noodles

These thin, gray-brown, dried Japanese noodles come in two types: those made with buckwheat flour, which are gluten-free; and those made with a combination of wheat and buckwheat, which are slightly more robust. There's also a version made with green tea powder, though the tea adds color rather than much flavor. When cooking soba, follow the instructions on the package to avoid the noodles overcooking and becoming sticky or even falling apart. When draining, follow the Japanese practice of reserving some of the cooking water. This is called sobayu and is sometimes added to the broth or dipping sauce or drunk as a soup. Refresh cooked noodles under cold running water to cool them quickly and get rid of excess starch. Soba can be served warm or cold in noodle salads or broths, or with a soy-based dipping sauce. They can be briefly stir-fried, but it's not ideal as they have a tendency to fall apart. If you want to reheat them, put them in a colander and pour a just-boiled kettleful of water over them — that should just be enough to warm them up.

Burma (Myanmar) is bordered by China, Thailand and India, so it's not unusual to find a mix of influences in a dish. Don't be put off by the list of ingredients; this fragrant curry is easy to make.

Burmese Noodle, Tofu and Winter Greens Curry

Serves: 4   **Preparation time:** *20 minutes, plus making the stock*
Cooking time: *25 minutes*

¼ cup mild curry powder
14 ounces firm tofu, drained, patted dry and
   cut into large bite-size cubes
1 onion, cut into wedges
3 large garlic cloves, peeled
1-inch piece of ginger root, peeled
   and quartered
¼ cup sunflower oil
1 x 14-ounce can coconut milk
1¼ cups Vegetable Stock (see page 14)
2 tablespoons light soy sauce

½ teaspoon dried red pepper flakes or
   1 medium red chili, sliced
2 lemongrass sticks, bruised
1 tablespoon brown sugar
1 red bell pepper, seeded and chopped
4 large handfuls of winter greens or curly
   kale, stalks removed, leaves shredded
7 ounces dried soba noodles
1 handful of cilantro, chopped
sea salt and freshly ground black pepper
lime wedges, to serve

1. Sprinkle half the curry powder over a plate and season with salt and pepper. Lightly dust the tofu in the curry powder and set to one side.

2. Put the onion, garlic, ginger and half the oil in a mini food processor and blend to a paste. Scrape the paste into a large, heavy pot and cook over medium heat 2 minutes, stirring continuously. Add the coconut milk, stock, soy sauce, red pepper flakes and lemongrass and bring up to boiling point, then stir in the sugar. Turn the heat down slightly and simmer, part-covered, 15 minutes until reduced and thickened. Add the remaining curry powder, the red bell pepper and the winter greens. Season with pepper, then cook, stirring occasionally, 5 minutes until tender.

3. Meanwhile, heat the remaining oil in a large, nonstick skillet and fry the tofu in two batches over medium heat 6 minutes, turning occasionally, until golden. Drain on paper towels. Cook the noodles following the package instructions, drain and divide into four large, shallow bowls. Spoon the curry over the top, followed by the tofu, and scatter with the cilantro before serving with wedges of lime.

Freeze any leftover coconut milk in ice cube trays or a plastic container with a lid. Tip out the cubes into a small plastic bag, secure the top and freeze up to 3 months.

Pictured on page 63.

►► Soba, Seaweed and Radish Salad

Cook **6 ounces dried soba noodles** following the package instructions, then drain and refresh under cold running water. Put them in a large serving bowl and add **¾ cup cooked and cooled edamame**, **10 thinly sliced radishes** and a **2½-inch piece seeded and cubed cucumber**. Lightly toast **1 tablespoon sesame seeds** and **3 tablespoons mixed seaweed salad** in a dry skillet 2 minutes, shaking the pan regularly, until the seaweed is crisp. To make the dressing, mix **¼ cup rice vinegar**, **2 teaspoons soy sauce**, **2 teaspoons sesame oil**, **⅓ cup sunflower oil**, **1 teaspoon peeled and finely chopped ginger root** and **1 small finely chopped garlic clove**. Season with **salt** and **pepper** and spoon the dressing over the noodle salad. Sprinkle with the vegetable mixture, and serve.

►► Soba with Miso Sauce

It's worth making double the quantity of this sauce, as it will keep up to 1 week in an airtight container in the refrigerator. Serve it warm or cold as a dressing for salads, a stir-fry sauce or spooned over cooked rice or pasta. Cook **8 ounces dried soba noodles** following the package instructions, then drain and refresh under cold running water. To make the sauce, combine **⅓ cup mirin** and **1 heaped tablespoon sugar** in a small pan and bring to a boil, then turn the heat down and simmer 2 minutes, stirring until the sugar dissolves. Mix together **⅓ cup plus 1 tablespoon water**, **¼ cup brown rice miso** and **1 tablespoon English mustard**, then stir into the pan. Pour boiling water over the noodles and divide into four large, shallow bowls, then pour the sauce over and turn until coated. Sprinkle with **chopped cilantro** and **toasted sesame seeds**, or serve with stir-fried vegetables or fried tofu.

►► Soba with Cilantro Dressing

Cook **9 ounces dried soba noodles** following the package instructions, then drain and refresh under cold running water. Combine **2 handfuls of fresh cilantro**, **2 large garlic cloves**, **1 long red chili**, **2-inch piece of peeled and chopped ginger root**, **finely grated zest and juice of 2 limes**, **⅓ cup sunflower oil**, **2 tablespoons light soy sauce**, **1 teaspoon sugar** and **1 tablespoon toasted sesame oil** in a mini food processor or blender and blend to a thick paste. Spoon the dressing over warm or cold noodles.

Chapter 3
Sack of Rice
(and Other Grains)

Reputedly the most widely eaten food on the planet, rice is so much more than just an accompaniment. There are numerous varieties to choose from, such as the creamy risotto rice used here in the Arancini Eggs, or jasmine rice, which goes to make the Thai Rice with Spiced Cashews. And let's not forget the numerous other grains, which are equally versatile and economical. Try them in the Barley, Squash and Wild Oregano Risotto or the Quinoa and Roasted Peanut Salad.

This is a cross between the Italian arancini (fried rice ball) and a meat-free version of the British Scotch egg. It came about when a friend gave me some eggs from her prolific hens and I had some leftover risotto in the refrigerator that needed eating. This marriage of dishes was pure guesswork, but I'm pleased to say that it's a happy union!

Arancini Eggs

Serves: *4*   **Preparation time:** *10 minutes*   **Cooking time:** *15 minutes*

5 eggs (1 lightly beaten)
3 tablespoons finely grated vegetarian
   parmesan cheese
3 cups leftover cooked risotto (or ⅓ recipe
   quantity Last-of-the-Beans Risotto, see
   page 81, leaving out the fava beans
   and Dolcelatte)

1 scant cup day-old breadcrumbs
¼ cup all-purpose flour
sunflower oil, for deep-frying
sea salt and freshly ground black pepper

1. Put 4 of the eggs in a pan of cold water and bring to a boil, then turn the heat down slightly and gently boil the eggs 5 minutes. Drain the eggs, cool under cold running water, then peel.

2. Meanwhile, stir the parmesan into the risotto rice and season with salt and pepper. Beat the remaining egg in a shallow bowl. Tip the breadcrumbs and flour each into two separate shallow bowls.

3. Take a quarter of the risotto mixture and press it out in an even layer in the palm of your hand. Lightly dust one of the eggs in the flour, then put it in the center of the risotto. Wrap the risotto around the egg in an even layer and press the edges together to make a ball. Dust the wrapped egg in the flour and pat away any excess, then dip into the beaten egg and roll in the breadcrumbs. Repeat to make 4 balls in total.

4. Heat oil in a deep pan to deep-fry the Arancini eggs. (It is hot enough when a piece of bread turns golden and crisp in 30 seconds.) Deep-fry 2 eggs at a time 4 to 5 minutes, turning them occasionally until golden and crisp. Drain on paper towels, and repeat to cook the other eggs. Serve warm.

Don't throw away leftover oil from deep-frying—instead, let it cool, then strain into an airtight jar and store in a dark, cool place. It can be used for up to 2 weeks. Alternatively, the oil can be poured into a freezer-proof container and frozen up to 3 months.

Radishes

are great for newcomers to vegetable growing, as they're easy to grow, tolerant of most soil types and take a mere 4 weeks to crop. They come in all shapes and sizes—from spherical to long and thin—and in colors ranging from red and cream to pink and white. Sow the seeds at weekly intervals for a ready supply of this crisp, slightly fiery vegetable throughout the summer.

With its nutty flavor and texture, buckwheat makes a more substantial addition to grain-based salads than couscous or quinoa. It's a bit of an intruder in the grain family, though, as it's actually a seed—however, it's often used in the same way as wheat so it deserves its place here.

Buckwheat and Sour Cherry Salad

Serves: 4 *Preparation time:* 15 minutes *Cooking time:* 25 minutes

heaped ¾ cup buckwheat groats or
   bulgur wheat
juice of ½ small orange
1 heaped teaspoon honey
3 tablespoons rice vinegar
1 handful of dried sour cherries, cut in half
   if large
6 radishes, cut into round slices

1 small red or pink onion, chopped
2 handfuls of mint leaves, chopped
2 handfuls of parsley leaves, chopped
2 tablespoons extra virgin olive oil
1 large handful of unsalted, shelled
   pistachios, toasted (see page 18)
1 scant cup feta cheese, crumbled
sea salt and freshly ground black pepper

1. Toast the buckwheat in a skillet over medium heat 3 minutes, turning the grains occasionally, until they smell toasted. Transfer to a saucepan and cover with water. Bring to a boil over medium heat, then turn the heat down to low and part-cover the pan. Cook 18 to 20 minutes, or until the buckwheat is soft, yet remains chewy.

2. Meanwhile, whisk the orange juice, honey and rice vinegar together in a small pan. Bring to a boil and add the sour cherries, then turn off the heat and let the cherries steep 15 minutes.

3. Drain the buckwheat well and tip into a serving bowl along with the radishes, onion, mint and parsley. Strain the sour cherries, reserving the juice mixture, and add them to the bowl. Whisk the olive oil into the juice mixture and pour it into the bowl, then season with salt and pepper. Toss the salad until combined, then scatter the pistachios and feta over the top just before serving at room temperature.

If you use nuts, seeds, grains and legumes regularly it's best to buy them in bulk—in large packs—to keep costs down. Do check the use-by date on a regular basis, though, as they will go stale over time.

This is almost an Asian version of tabbouleh. As with the classic tabbouleh, its success lies in getting the balance right between the grain and the flavorings. The herbs should be dominant, as the cilantro is here; a very high proportion of grains makes for a dull salad. I love the combination of crisp onions and ginger, roasted peanuts and soft herbs with the slightly salty soy dressing. I've used red quinoa for its color more than anything else; go for whichever type you can buy easily.

Quinoa and Roasted Peanut Salad

Serves: 4   **Preparation time:** 10 minutes   **Cooking time:** 10 minutes

⅓ cup red quinoa
1 tablespoon canola oil
heaped ⅓ cup whole unsalted peanuts
1 large handful of cilantro, leaves and
   stalks finely chopped
1 tablespoon sesame seeds, toasted
   (see page 18)
3 tablespoons Crispy Onions and Ginger
   (see page 23)

DRESSING
1 teaspoon tamari or light soy sauce
2 tablespoons canola oil
½ teaspoon sugar
sea salt and freshly ground black pepper

1. Put the quinoa in a pan, cover with water and bring to a boil. Turn the heat down and simmer, part-covered, 10 minutes until tender. Drain and set to one side.

2. Meanwhile, heat the oil in a large skillet over medium heat. Turn the heat to medium-low, add the peanuts and fry 2 to 3 minutes, turning once, until toasted. Remove with a slotted spoon, drain on paper towels and let cool.

3. Mix together the ingredients for the dressing and season with salt and pepper. Put the cilantro leaves and stalks in a bowl along with the quinoa, peanuts and sesame seeds. Pour the dressing over them and toss until combined. Serve with the Crispy Onions and Ginger sprinkled over the top.

Serve with the Pea and Tofu Fritters (see page 162).

Don't discard the stalks from cilantro or parsley, as they contain plenty of flavor and can be added to dishes where a slight crunch is not an issue, such as in this salad.

This is so adaptable. Go easy on the additions and serve it as a side dish to the Moroccan Slow-Cooked Vegetables (see page 159) or with the Pomegranate Salsa (see page 21), or pimp it up with extra cheese or a fried egg to make a main meal.

Feta and Pumpkin Seed Pilaf

Serves: 4   **Preparation time:** 15 minutes, plus making the stock and 10 minutes standing   **Cooking time:** 25 minutes

2 tablespoons sunflower oil
1 onion, finely chopped
3 garlic cloves, finely chopped
8 cloves
6 cardamom pods, split
1 tablespoon cumin seeds
½ teaspoon dried red pepper flakes
1¾ cups basmati rice
1 heaped teaspoon turmeric
3¼ cups Vegetable Stock, plus extra
   if needed (see page 14)

3 handfuls of spinach, tough stalks
   removed, leaves shredded
1 cup drained canned lima beans
   or cooked dried lima beans
   (see pages 8–9)
3 tablespoons pumpkin seeds, toasted
   (see page 18)
1 scant cup feta cheese, crumbled
sea salt and freshly ground black pepper

1. Heat the oil in a medium, deep skillet over medium heat. Add the onion and fry 6 minutes until softened, then add the garlic, cloves, cardamom, cumin and red pepper flakes and cook 2 minutes.

2. Stir in the rice and turmeric, then pour in the stock; it should cover the rice by about ½ inch. Bring to a boil, then turn the heat down to its lowest setting, cover with a lid and and cook 5 minutes.

3. Briefly remove the lid and stir in the spinach and lima beans, then return the lid and cook another 10 minutes, or until the rice is tender and the stock has been absorbed. (Add more stock if the rice is not cooked, cover with the lid again and cook a few more minutes until tender.) Season to taste with salt and pepper and let stand 10 minutes. Serve the rice in bowls, sprinkled with the pumpkin seeds and feta cheese.

Leftover cooked rice can be kept in the refrigerator up to 2 days or frozen; either way make sure you reheat it really well.

This is my take on the signature Korean rice dish, traditionally topped with seven different vegetables and a raw egg, which cooks in the heat of the rice. I like to vary the vegetables and prefer a soft-boiled egg or thin strips of omelet. A spoonful of Kimchi (see page 20) is not to be forgotten!

Bibimbap

Serves: *4* **Preparation time:** *20 minutes, plus making the stock*
Cooking time: *20 minutes*

2 cups short-grain brown rice, rinsed
4 large eggs
2 tablespoons vegetable oil
9 ounces crimini mushrooms, sliced
2 carrots, cut into thin strips
2 zucchini, cut into thin strips
7 ounces young spinach leaves, tough
  stalks removed
5 scallions, finely chopped

3 garlic cloves, finely chopped
1 tablespoon sesame seeds, toasted
  (see page 18)
3 tablespoons light soy sauce
1 teaspoon sesame oil
1 cup Vegetable Stock (see page 14)
sea salt and freshly ground black pepper
Kimchi (see page 20), to serve

1. Put the rice in a pot, pour in enough cold water to cover by ½ inch and season with salt. Bring to a boil, then turn the heat down to its lowest setting and cover. Simmer 20 minutes, or until the rice is tender and the water has been absorbed. Let the rice stand on the warm stove until ready to serve.

2. Meanwhile, soft-boil the eggs 4 minutes in a small pan, cool briefly under cold running water, then peel and set to one side. While the eggs are cooking, heat the vegetable oil in a large wok over high heat and stir-fry the mushrooms 4 minutes until starting to turn golden. Set to one side.

3. Steam the carrots and zucchini 2 to 3 minutes, keeping them separate, until just tender. Cook the spinach with a splash of water 2 to 3 minutes until tender. Transfer all the vegetables to a large, warm plate and cover to keep them warm.

4. Put the scallions, garlic, sesame seeds, soy sauce, sesame oil and vegetable stock in a small pan and simmer over medium-low heat 2 minutes, then season with pepper.

5. Divide the rice into four warm bowls and spoon over it two thirds of the hot stock mixture. Top with the vegetables, keeping each one in a separate pile. Spoon the remaining stock mixture over the top. Cut each egg in half and put in the center. Serve immediately with the Kimchi.

I always keep a bag of frozen spinach in the freezer. Look for whole-leaf spinach rather than chopped, which has a tendency to turn to mush when cooked.

Calendula (pot marigold) was once known as "poor man's saffron," as its dried petals look remarkably similar to strands of saffron but at a fraction of the price. Soak the dried petals briefly to release their golden color.

Paella with Poor Man's Saffron

Serves: 4   *Preparation time:* 15 minutes, plus making the stock, 30 minutes soaking and 10 minutes standing   *Cooking time:* 35 minutes

2 heaped teaspoons dried pot marigold petals
   (see opposite)
1½ cups frozen baby peas
3 tablespoons canola or olive oil
1 large onion, chopped
2 large peppers, 1 red and 1 yellow, seeded
   and chopped
3 garlic cloves, chopped
1½ cups paella rice
2 teaspoons smoked mild paprika
1 teaspoon turmeric

¼ cup sherry, or extra vegetable stock
5 cups Vegetable Stock (see page 14)
2 tomatoes, seeded and chopped
2 handfuls of small black pitted olives
sea salt and freshly ground black pepper

SMOKED PAPRIKA ALMONDS
1 tablespoon canola or olive oil
½ cup blanched whole almonds
1 heaping teaspoon smoked mild paprika

1. Soak the marigold petals in ¼ cup warm water 30 minutes. Meanwhile, let the peas defrost in a bowl. Heat the oil in a paella pan or large, nonstick, deep skillet with a lid, over medium heat. Add the onion and fry 5 minutes until softened but not colored. Add the peppers and cook another 3 minutes, then add the garlic and cook until the peppers have softened.

2. Add the rice, smoked paprika and turmeric and turn to coat them in the onions. Pour in the sherry, if using, and let it bubble away until the alcohol evaporates, then pour in the stock and marigold petals and soaking liquid, season with salt and pepper, stir and bring to a boil. Turn the heat down to low and let the rice cook without stirring for 15 minutes.

3. Scatter over it the peas, tomatoes and olives and press into the rice with the back of a spoon. Do not stir the rice; you want the bottom to form a crust. Cook another 5 minutes until the rice is tender and the stock mostly absorbed. Remove from the heat, cover and let stand 10 minutes.

4. Meanwhile, heat the oil in a skillet over medium heat and fry the almonds 3 minutes, shaking occasionally, until they start to color. Add the paprika and season with salt, turn the nuts to coat and cook another 2 minutes. Tip out onto a plate. Serve the paella scattered with the paprika almonds.

Poor man's saffron is also used in Moroccan Slow-Cooked Vegetables (see page 159).

Pot marigolds (calendula) are easy to grow, require little maintenance and bring color to the garden. Not only are the flowers edible, they also act as a natural insect repellent, avoiding the need for pesticide sprays. To dry the flowers, remove the petals from the flower heads and spread out on a baking sheet, then leave overnight until dried and store in an airtight container.

Couscous makes a great base for stuffings as it takes on the flavors of stronger ingredients and adds substance. Here, it is mixed with harissa, which also doubles up as the flavoring of the sauce. Use large mushrooms with a slightly raised edge, which act like a bowl to hold the stuffing.

Roasted Mushrooms with Couscous Crust

Serves: *4* **Preparation time:** *15 minutes, plus making the stock*
Cooking time: *35 minutes*

heaped ⅓ cup couscous
hot Vegetable Stock (see page 14), to cover
3 tablespoons olive oil, plus extra for drizzling
1 onion, finely chopped
2 large garlic cloves, finely chopped
1 tablespoon harissa paste
1 teaspoon smoked mild paprika
1 large handful of flat-leaf parsley leaves,
  chopped
1 large handful of oregano leaves, chopped

4 large portobello or field mushrooms,
  stalks discarded
1 cup rindless goat cheese, crumbled
sea salt and freshly ground black pepper
mixed salad greens, to serve

HARISSA MAYO
1 heaped teaspoon harissa
⅓ cup plus 1 tablespoon mayonnaise
juice of ½ lemon

1. Preheat the oven to 375°F. Put the couscous in a heatproof bowl and pour over it enough hot stock to just cover. Stir, cover with a plate to keep in the heat and leave 5 minutes, or until the stock is absorbed. Fluff up the couscous with a fork to separate the grains.

2. Meanwhile, heat half the oil in a large skillet over medium heat. Add the onion and fry 8 minutes until softened but not colored. Add the garlic and cook another minute. Add the harissa, paprika, cooked couscous and half the herbs, season with salt and pepper and stir until combined.

3. Brush the tops (not the gills) and edges of each mushroom with the remaining oil and put them in a small roasting pan to keep them upright. Spoon the couscous mixture in a pile on top, pressing it down slightly, then pour in 1 tablespoon water, cover with foil and roast 15 minutes until the mushrooms have softened. Remove the foil, scatter the goat cheese over the top of each one, drizzle with a little oil and return to the oven another 10 minutes until the cheese has melted slightly.

4. Meanwhile, mix together all the ingredients for the harissa mayo with 1 to 2 tablespoons warm water and salt and pepper. Serve the mushrooms, sprinkled with the remaining herbs, with the harissa mayo and salad.

To dry robust herbs, such as rosemary, oregano, sage and thyme, put a single layer between two sheets of paper towels and microwave 1 to 3 minutes.

This stir-fried rice dish is perfect for a weekday dinner. You could cook the rice the day before, but do reheat it thoroughly. You don't have to add the cashews, but I like their crunch in contrast to the softness of the rice.

Thai Rice with Spiced Cashews

Serves: 4 **Preparation time:** 20 minutes, plus cooling
Cooking time: 20 minutes

2¼ cups Thai jasmine rice
3 tablespoons sunflower oil
4 large scallions, sliced, green and white
    parts kept separate
2 bok choy, white parts thinly sliced
    and green leaves thickly sliced and
    kept separate
2 lemongrass stalks, outer leaves removed
    and finely chopped
1 red chili, finely chopped
1½-inch piece of ginger root, finely chopped

4 garlic cloves, finely chopped
3 tablespoons light soy sauce
juice of ½ lime
1 teaspoon sugar
1 small handful of basil leaves, preferably
    Thai, to serve

SPICED CASHEWS
⅔ cup cashews
2 teaspoons Thai 7-spice
2 teaspoons soy sauce

1. Put the rice in a medium saucepan and pour in enough cold water to cover by ½ inch. Bring to a boil, then turn the heat down to its lowest setting and cover with a lid. Simmer about 12 minutes, or until the water has been absorbed and the rice is tender. Turn off the heat and leave the rice to stand, still covered, 5 minutes. Spread out the rice on a large plate and let cool.

2. Meanwhile, preheat the oven to 315°F. Put the cashews on a baking sheet and toast 12 minutes, turning halfway. Mix together the 7-spice and soy sauce in a bowl. Add the toasted cashews and stir until coated in the spice mixture. Tip the nuts back onto the baking sheet and return to the oven another 3 minutes until crisp. Remove and set to one side.

3. Heat the oil in a wok over high heat. Add the white part of the scallion and bok choy and stir-fry 2 minutes, then add the lemongrass, chili, green part of the bok choy, ginger and garlic and stir-fry another 1 minute. Add the cooked, cooled rice and stir-fry 3 minutes, or until piping hot. Mix together the soy sauce, lime juice and sugar until the sugar dissolves, then pour into the wok. Toss until combined and spoon onto plates. Scatter over it the green part of the scallions, the basil and the spiced cashews.

Thai 7-spice is also used in Crispy Thai-Spiced Tofu (see page 43).

If you have a large bag of nuts that you know won't be eaten right away, freeze them in ziploc bags. There's no need to defrost them before using.

This risotto came about when I had just a handful of homegrown fava beans left—not enough to serve on their own. Fava beans are perfect with blue cheese, especially a creamy Dolcelatte, and there's no need for the usual addition, parmesan, as this dish is plenty cheesy enough.

Last-of-the-Beans Risotto

Serves: 4   **Preparation time:** *10 minutes, plus making the stock and 10 minutes standing*   **Cooking time:** *25 minutes*

2 cups shelled fresh or frozen fava beans
2 tablespoons butter
1 tablespoon olive oil
1 large leek, finely chopped
1¾ cups risotto rice
½ cup dry white wine or extra vegetable stock

5 cups hot Vegetable Stock (see page 14)
6 ounces Dolcelatte, chopped into bite-size chunks (or Gorgonzola)
1 tablespoon chopped flat-leaf parsley leaves
sea salt and freshly ground black pepper

1. Cook the fava beans in a pan of boiling water about 3 minutes until just tender. Drain and refresh under cold running water, then remove the beans from their tough outer skins and set to one side. Discard the tough outer skins.

2. Meanwhile, heat the butter and oil in a large, heavy pan. When melted, add the leek and sauté gently 6 minutes until tender. Stir in the rice, and when coated in the buttery leeks, pour in the wine, if using. Let the wine bubble away until the alcohol evaporates and then start to add the stock, a ladleful at a time, stirring constantly. Only add the next ladleful when the previous one has been absorbed by the rice, and continue until the rice is creamy with just a slight bite. The rice should be slightly soupy, not dry, and takes about 25 minutes to cook in total.

3. When the rice is cooked, season with pepper and stir in the fava beans and Dolcelatte. Cover with a lid and let stand 10 minutes. Taste, and add a little salt, if needed, before serving sprinkled with parsley.

Leftover risotto rice can be used for Arancini Eggs (see page 68). Stir in 3 tablespoons grated vegetarian parmesan instead of the broad beans and Dolcelatte.

Barley is such an underrated grain and is enormously versatile, lending a creaminess and slightly chewy texture to chunky soups and stews, and substance to salads and pilafs. It also makes an economical alternative to risotto rice.

Barley, Squash and Wild Oregano Risotto

Serves: 4 *Preparation time:* 15 minutes, plus making the stock
Cooking time: 50 minutes

1½ ounces butternut squash, peeled, seeded
   and cut into large bite-size pieces
1 bulb garlic, cloves separated but not peeled
1 handful of wild oregano or marjoram
¼ cup olive oil
3 tablespoons butter
1 large onion, finely chopped

1 long red chili, finely chopped, not seeded
1½ cups barley, rinsed
1 cup dry white wine or extra
   vegetable stock
3½ cups hot Vegetable Stock
   (see page 14)
sea salt and freshly ground black pepper

1. Preheat the oven to 375°F. Toss the squash, garlic cloves and 3 sprigs of the oregano in half the oil in a large roasting pan and roast 20 minutes until the garlic has softened. Remove the garlic and oregano, turn the squash and return to the oven another 10 to 15 minutes until tender and golden in places. Meanwhile, peel and roughly chop the garlic and set to one side.

2. Remove the leaves from the remaining oregano, reserving 1 teaspoon, and put the rest in a small blender with the remaining olive oil and blend to make a herb oil. Set to one side.

3. While the squash is roasting, melt the butter in a large, heavy pan over medium heat. Add the onion and three quarters of the chili and sauté covered, 8 minutes, until softened but not colored. Add the barley and cook 2 minutes, stirring to coat the grains in the buttery onions, and then pour in the wine, if using. Let the wine bubble away until absorbed by the grains, then stir in the hot vegetable stock all at once. Stir well until combined and simmer over medium-low heat, part-covered, 30 to 40 minutes until the grains are tender but still retain a slight bite.

4. Season with salt and pepper and stir in the herb oil, roasted squash and roasted garlic. Add a splash more stock or water, since you don't want the risotto to be too dry. Serve seasoned with extra pepper and sprinkled with the reserved oregano and chili.

You'll be able to smell *wild* *oregano* before you spot it. This aromatic fresh herb loves grassy, chalky soil. The slightly downy leaves have pink or white flower heads, which are also edible. Oregano comes from the same family as marjoram and so I use these herbs interchangeably in cooking. In fact, you may be able to find wild marjoram in similar places, too.

☞ Polenta

The beauty of polenta (cornmeal), the golden-yellow ground corn, is that it's versatile and a great carrier of flavors — and it's cheap. Polenta is not just a staple in Northern Italy, where it's principally a winter food served as a type of savory porridge with stews, it's also popular in the southern US states, where it's grown to make grits and cornbread. It makes a welcome alternative to carbs such as rice, pasta, bread and potatoes, and may come ground or in slabs for frying or broiling. The coarser the grain, the longer it takes to cook and the stronger your arm will have to be for all the stirring. Instant polenta (cornmeal) cuts the cooking time to about 5 to 10 minutes. Use polenta as an alternative to mashed potatoes, to make a crust for a quiche, fried in cubes for croûtons, as crumbs for coating croquettes or in baking. For a flavor boost, add butter, cheese, herbs or chili.

▶▶

Broiled wedges of polenta with their soft, yielding interior and crisp, golden crust make an excellent alternative to toasted bread. Flavored simply with parmesan and chili, the bruschetta go well served with the Moroccan Slow-Cooked Vegetables on page 159. Try experimenting with different flavorings, such as black olives, herbs, spices, sundried tomatoes, char-broiled eggplants or artichokes. Polenta freezes well—just prepare it up to the point it is cut into triangles, then freeze in individual pieces on a baking sheet. When frozen, transfer the polenta to a ziploc bag for storing, then simply defrost and broil when ready to eat.

Polenta Bruschetta

Serves: *4–6*   **Preparation time:** *10 minutes, plus 30 minutes chilling*
Cooking time: *20 minutes*

scant 1¼ cups instant polenta
3 tablespoons butter, cubed
¾ cup vegetarian parmesan cheese,
   finely grated
1 teaspoon dried red pepper flakes

1 teaspoon sea salt
olive oil, for brushing
1 recipe quantity Moroccan Slow-Cooked
   Vegetables (see page 159), to serve

1. Heat 3½ cups water in a pan over medium-low heat and when warm, gradually stir in the polenta. Bring to a boil, then turn the heat down to low and simmer, stirring, 10 minutes until thick and smooth; take care as it can splatter. Remove the pan from the heat and stir in the butter, parmesan, red pepper flakes and salt.

2. Lightly grease a large baking tray and spread the polenta into an even layer about ¾ inch thick, then let cool and place in the refrigerator to set. This will take about 30 minutes.

3. Preheat the broiler to high (or you could use a ridged grill pan). Cut the polenta slab into 4 squares, then each one diagonally into a triangle. Brush one side of the polenta with oil and broil 3 to 4 minutes until crisp and golden on the outside. Brush the top of the polenta with more oil, turn it over and broil another 3 to 4 minutes. Serve with the Moroccan Slow-Cooked Vegetables.

Pictured on page 85.

▶▶ Cheesy Chili Cornbread

Preheat the oven to 375°F and **butter** a 2-pound loaf pan. Mix together **1 heaped cup instant polenta**, **½ cup plus 1 tablespoon all-purpose flour**, **2 teaspoons baking powder**, **½ teaspoon baking soda**, **1 teaspoon sea salt**, **1 teaspoon English mustard powder**, **1 seeded and chopped red chili** and **¾ cup sharp cheddar cheese, grated**, in a large mixing bowl. Melt **¼ cup butter** and combine with **2 large beaten eggs**, **1 cup minus 2 tablespoons buttermilk** and **3 tablespoons milk**. Add the wet ingredients to the dry ingredients and pour into the prepared pan. Bake 35 to 40 minutes, or until golden and a skewer inserted into the middle comes out clean.

▶▶ Soft Polenta

Pour **2 cups Vegetable Stock** (see page 14) and **¾ cup milk** into a saucepan and bring to a boil. Add **1 heaped cup instant polenta** in a steady stream, stirring continuously, season with salt and pepper and cook 5 minutes until it is the consistency of soft mashed potato.

▶▶ Polenta Crust for Quiche

Follow the ingredients and method for **Polenta Bruschetta**, opposite. After making, let it cool about 5 minutes until it starts to firm up slightly. Spoon the polenta into a 10-inch removable-bottomed fluted tart pan that has been greased with **olive oil**. Spread the polenta evenly over the bottom and up the sides to a thickness of about ¼ inch; there will be some left over, which can be used to patch up any cracks that appear. Preheat the oven to 350°F and bake 30 minutes, or until firm and crisp. Fill the polenta crust with the filling of your choice.

Chapter 4
Bag of Nuts
(and Seeds)

Delicious as a snack, nuts also make a valuable, nutritious
and sustaining base to a meal, whether it be a light and
summery Pecan, Pear and Nasturtium Salad, warming fall
Chestnut and Mushroom Pie, a twist on the classic Italian
dumplings in the form of Semolina and Nut Milk Gnocchi,
or festive-inspired Roasted Onions with Nut Stuffing.
Similarly, the unassuming seed is transformed into a creamy,
spiced Tahini and Squash Dip, Sesame and Nori Cakes,
or delicious puff-pastry Pumpkin Seed Rolls.

A jar of tahini is surprisingly versatile: hummus wouldn't be hummus without it, and a spoonful stirred into a miso stock makes a rich broth. I like to add a little to a soy-ginger dressing or use it as a healthier alternative to butter. Here, the sesame seed paste is turned into an addictive butternut squash dip, served with spicy flatbread crisps.

Tahini and Squash Dip

Serves: 6   **Preparation time:** 15 minutes, plus making the yogurt and cooling
Cooking time: 45 minutes

2¼ pounds butternut squash, peeled, seeded
   and cut into bite-size chunks
3 tablespoons olive oil, plus extra for brushing
1 teaspoon ground allspice
½ cup Wholemilk Yogurt (see page 16) or
   Greek yogurt
heaped ¼ cup tablespoons light tahini paste
juice of 1 lemon
2 garlic cloves, crushed

2 teaspoons pomegranate molasses (optional)
1 tablespoon sesame seeds, toasted
   (see page 18)
1 small handful of cilantro leaves, chopped
sea salt and freshly ground black pepper

FLATBREAD CRISPS
6 round flatbreads
2 tablespoons Dukka (see page 109)

1. Preheat the oven to 350°F. Put the squash in a large bowl and add the oil and allspice. Season well with salt and pepper and turn the squash with your hands until coated in the seasoned oil. Tip the squash onto a large cookie sheet (or you may need two) and spread it out into an even layer. Roast 45 minutes, turning once, or until tender and slightly golden on the edges. Let cool.

2. While the squash is roasting, use the heat of the oven to make the flatbread crisps. Brush one of the flatbreads with a little oil and put it in the oven with the roasting squash 4 to 5 minutes, or until light golden and crisp; keep an eye on it, as it burns easily. Remove from the oven, brush with more oil and sprinkle 1 teaspoon of the dukka over them, then repeat until you have prepared all 6 flatbreads. Pile on top of one another and set to one side.

3. Put the roasted, cooled squash in a large bowl and add the yogurt, tahini, lemon juice, garlic and half the pomegranate molasses, if using, then mash with a potato masher to a coarse paste. You can do this in a food processor if you prefer a smoother dip. Season with salt and pepper. Drizzle the remaining pomegranate molasses over the top and sprinkle with the sesame seeds and cilantro.
   Serve with the flatbread crisps.

Serve with Eggplant Meze (see page 158).

Keep flatbreads fresh by storing them in the freezer, then reheat under the broiler or in a toaster, from frozen, when you need them.

Cut-and-come-again salad seeds are widely available and easy to grow, so it's feasible to have a constant supply of mixed greens throughout the summer months—and even into the winter if in a sheltered spot. Look for a seed mixture that gives you a range of colors and textures, then simply harvest the leaves regularly to encourage new growth.

If I'm going to be using chopped walnuts in a recipe, I prefer to buy walnut pieces—not only do they save me the bother of chopping them, they are also much cheaper than the whole or halved equivalents. I steer clear of turning the oven on just to roast a small amount of nuts, so it makes sense to plan ahead, if you can, and utilize the oven for more than one dish.

Toasted Walnut Salad

Serves: 4   **Preparation time:** 10 minutes   **Cooking time:** 4 minutes

1 head of broccoli, large stalk removed,
   cut into small florets
3 handfuls of oakleaf or other red salad
   leaves, torn into large pieces
1½ cups drained canned green lentils or
   cooked dried green lentils (see page 9)
½ red onion, chopped
2 cooked beets, cubed
1 handful of shredded red cabbage

2 handfuls of walnut pieces, toasted
   (see page 18)

DRESSING
¼ cup extra virgin olive oil
2 tablespoons balsamic vinegar, plus extra
   if needed
1 teaspoon honey
sea salt and freshly ground black pepper

1. Cook the broccoli florets in a pan of boiling salted water 4 minutes until only just tender. Refresh under cold running water and let drain and cool.

2. Mix together the ingredients for the dressing—adding more balsamic vinegar if you like a sharper dressing—and season with salt and pepper.

3. Put the salad leaves on a large serving plate and scatter the lentils, red onion, beets, red cabbage and cooked broccoli over them. Spoon the dressing on top and toss lightly until combined, adding more salt and pepper if necessary. Scatter the walnuts over the top just before serving.

Serve with the Pumpkin Seed Rolls (see page 97).

Don't throw the broccoli stalk away; instead cut it into thin sticks and combine with strips of carrot and cabbage. Coat the vegetables in a mustardy mayonnaise dressing for an excellent twist on coleslaw.

The secret to the success of this vibrant salad is the combination of texture, color and flavor. The sweet caramelized pears are perfect with the salty sharpness of the blue cheese, the peppery freshness of the leaves and the crunch of the toasted pecans. You can, of course, vary the combination to suit but do keep in mind the blend of salty, sweet, soft and crunch.

Pecan, Pear and Nasturtium Salad

Serves: 4   Preparation time: 15 minutes   Cooking time: 5 minutes

1 tablespoon butter
2 slightly under-ripe pears, peeled, cored
  and each cut into 8 wedges
1 teaspoon ground ginger
1 tablespoon honey
5 ounces watercress
1 handful of nasturtium leaves and flowers
1 small red onion, thinly sliced
2 cooked beets, cubed

2 handfuls of pecan halves, toasted
  (see page 18)
3½ ounces crumbly blue cheese (about 1 cup)

DRESSING
3 tablespoons extra virgin olive oil
1 tablespoon white wine vinegar
1 teaspoon Dijon mustard
sea salt and freshly ground black pepper

1. Melt the butter in a large, nonstick skillet and cook the pears over medium heat 4 minutes, turning once, until softened. Stir in the ginger and honey, turn the pears to coat them in the syrupy mixture and cook another minute.

2. Meanwhile, make the dressing. Whisk together the olive oil, vinegar and mustard and season with salt and pepper.

3. Divide the watercress and nasturtium leaves onto four serving plates. Top with the red onion and beets and drizzle the dressing over them. Turn gently to coat the salad in the dressing, then top with the pecans, blue cheese, pears and nasturtium flowers before serving.

Not only do they look extremely attractive in the garden with their cheery colored petals, nasturtiums have both **edible** *leaves and edible flowers.* They are easy and undemanding plants to grow. The leaves have a peppery heat, while the flowers taste spicy and slightly sweet. They are both great in salads, valued for their taste as well as their looks.

This Roman version of gnocchi is made with semolina instead of the usual potato, and is baked in the oven. Don't waste any remnants of dough—they will keep in the refrigerator a day or so and can be rolled into balls (then breadcrumbed, or not) and shallow-fried until crisp. As an alternative to the eggplant sauce, you can layer the gnocchi in an ovenproof dish, cover with your favorite pasta sauce and mozzarella and bake in the oven.

Semolina and Nut Milk Gnocchi

Serves: 4   Preparation time: 10 minutes, plus overnight chilling
Cooking time: 30 minutes

2 tablespoons butter, melted, plus extra
   for greasing
2 cups unsweetened almond or cashew milk
1 teaspoon sea salt
¼ teaspoon freshly ground black pepper
1 heaped cup semolina

2 large eggs, lightly beaten
1¼ cups vegetarian parmesan cheese,
   finely grated
1 recipe quantity Eggplant Meze
   (see page 158), to serve

1. Line a large baking tray with wax paper and grease with butter. Pour the nut milk into a medium-sized pan, stir in the salt and pepper and bring it almost to a boil over medium heat. Gradually add the semolina, stirring constantly with a wooden spoon, then turn the heat down to low and cook the semolina 5 minutes, stirring, until you have a very thick paste. It will start to come away from the sides of the pan and be difficult to stir, but keep going for the full cooking time.

2. Remove the pan from the heat and beat in the eggs, 1 cup of the parmesan and one tablespoon of butter. Spoon the mixture onto the prepared baking tray and, using a rubber spatula, spread it out into an even layer about ½-inch thick. Occasionally dunk the spatula into water to stop the mixture sticking. Cover with a sheet of greased wax paper and let cool (ideally, put it in the refrigerator overnight to firm up).

3. Preheat the oven to 400°F and line a cookie sheet with baking parchment. Cut the semolina into 16 × 2½-inch circles using a cookie cutter and place on the cookie sheet. Brush the gnocchi with the remaining melted butter and sprinkle with the rest of the parmesan. Bake 25 minutes, or until slightly risen and golden. Serve with the Eggplant Meze (page 158).

Make double the quantity and freeze uncooked gnocchi on a lined cookie sheet. When frozen, transfer to a ziploc bag. Defrost before baking.

I like to keep store-bought puff pastry dough in the freezer, as it makes a quick and convenient bottom—or topping—for sweet or savory pies, tarts and galettes. This is my vegetarian version of the ever-popular British sausage roll.

Pumpkin Seed Rolls

Serves: 10   *Preparation time:* 15 minutes, plus 30 minutes chilling
Cooking time: 40 minutes

2 tablespoons olive oil
1 large onion, finely chopped
5½ ounces chestnut (or crimini) mushrooms, finely chopped
¼ cup pumpkin seeds
½ cup finely chopped sundried tomatoes
2½ cups fresh breadcrumbs
2 teaspoons harissa
finely grated zest of 1 lemon

2 eggs
1 tablespoon thyme leaves or 2 teaspoons dried thyme
all-purpose flour, for dusting
14-ounce block frozen puff pastry dough, defrosted and cut in half
1 tablespoon sesame seeds
sea salt and freshly ground black pepper

1. To make the filling, heat the oil in a large skillet over medium heat. Add the onion and fry 5 minutes until softened, then add the mushrooms and cook another 5 minutes until tender. Stir in the pumpkin seeds and cook 3 minutes, stirring occasionally, until they start to pop and smell toasted. Add the sundried tomatoes and let cool a little before transferring to a mini food processor and blitzing to a coarse paste.

2. Transfer the paste to a bowl and stir in the breadcrumbs, harissa, lemon zest, 1 of the eggs, and the thyme. Season with salt and pepper, then stir well until combined. Let cool.

3. Beat the remaining egg in a bowl. Lightly dust a work surface with flour and roll out the pastry dough into 2 × 15 × 6-inch sheets, about ¼ inch thick. Divide the filling mixture in half and spoon one half down the long side of each pastry sheet. Using your hands, shape the filling into 2 long sausages, pressing the mixture to encourage it to hold together. Brush the edges of the pastry sheets with the beaten egg. Fold the dough over the filling and press the edges together to make 2 tight rolls. Trim the edges, crimp with a fork and cut each roll into 5 pieces. Using a small knife, make light diagonal cuts on top of each roll, then brush the tops with beaten egg.

4. Put the rolls on a flour-dusted, nonstick cookie sheet and chill 30 minutes. Preheat the oven to 425°F. Remove the cookie sheet from the refrigerator, brush the rolls with more egg and sprinkle with sesame seeds. Bake 20 to 25 minutes until risen and golden, then let cool slightly before serving.

Sundried tomatoes are also used in Pizzata (see page 119).

You could make use of any leftover pastry dough, and the hot oven, to make "cheese straws."

*Great as an appetizer or a light meal, these light, fluffy Chinese buns
have a filling of hoisin, cashews and mushrooms. Surplus uncooked buns
can be frozen on a cookie sheet, then transferred to a freezer bag.*

Yum Cha Buns

Makes: *8 large buns*   **Preparation time:** *30 minutes, plus about 2 hours rising*
Cooking time: *15 minutes, or more if cooking in batches*

2 teaspoons dried yeast
2 teaspoons sugar
1½ cups all-purpose flour, plus extra
    for dusting
½ teaspoon salt
¾ teaspoon baking powder
1½ tablespoons sunflower oil, plus extra
    for greasing

CASHEW FILLING
7 ounces crimini mushrooms, finely chopped
1-inch piece of ginger root, peeled and very
    finely chopped
3 tablespoons hoisin sauce, plus extra
    to serve
3 scallions, finely chopped
⅓ cup toasted cashews (see page 18),
    finely chopped
freshly ground black pepper

1. To make the dough, pour ½ cup tepid water into a small bowl and sprinkle the yeast and sugar over it. Stir until the sugar dissolves, then leave it 10 minutes until frothy. Sift the flour, salt and baking powder into a large mixing bowl, stir and make a well in the center. Pour the yeast mixture and 1½ teaspoons of the oil into the well and gradually mix in the flour to form a soft ball of dough. Turn out onto a lightly floured work surface and knead 10 minutes until you have a smooth and elastic ball of dough. Clean the mixing bowl and wipe the inside with a little oil. Add the dough, cover the bowl with plastic wrap and leave in a warm place until doubled in size, about 2 hours.

2. Meanwhile, make the filling. Heat a wok over high heat, add the remaining oil and stir-fry the mushrooms and ginger 8 minutes, or until any liquid evaporates. Spoon the mixture into a bowl and stir in the hoisin, scallions and cashews. Season with pepper, and set to one side.

3. Turn the dough out onto a lightly floured surface. Divide into 8 balls and cover with a damp lintfree dish towel. Take a dough ball and press it into a circle about ¼ inch thick, then put a heaped tablespoonful of the mushroom mixture in the center of the dough and pull the edges up over the filling, pressing them together to seal. Place on a lightly floured surface and repeat with remaining balls and filling.

4. Put the buns in a tiered steamer, lined with baking parchment or wax paper. Cover with a lid and steam 15 minutes, or until risen and fluffy. (You can cook the buns in batches, if necessary.) Serve the buns warm with extra hoisin sauce for dipping.

Grow *rainbow chard,* and you will not only be rewarded with dazzling magenta, orange, red and yellow stalks topped with verdant leaves, but you can keep a steady supply throughout the summer and well into the winter months. Simply harvest the outer leaves to allow new growth. The small, young leaves can be eaten in salads, while more established leaves are good braised, steamed or stir-fried.

Here, the most simple of ingredients are turned into something special with very little effort. The baked onions are served simply with steamed rainbow chard, but they would also be delicious with a cauliflower puree made by boiling the florets in vegetable stock, then blending them with a little light cream and salt and pepper.

Roasted Onions with Nut Stuffing

Serves: *4*   **Preparation time:** *10 minutes*   **Cooking time:** *1 hour 15 minutes*

4 onions, unpeeled
4 thick slices of country-style bread
¼ cup olive oil
4 teaspoons balsamic vinegar
sea salt and freshly ground black pepper
steamed rainbow chard, to serve

NUT STUFFING
heaped ⅓ cup blanched almonds, toasted
  (see page 18)
scant ⅓ cup sunflower seeds, toasted
  (see page 18)
3 tablespoons day-old breadcrumbs
finely grated zest of 1 lemon
¼ cup chopped flat-leaf parsley leaves
2 tablespoons chopped rosemary or
  sage leaves

1. Preheat the oven to 350°F. Trim the root end of each onion so it stands up and then slice a cross into the top, cutting about halfway down. Remove any loose skin from the onions, put each one on a slice of bread and transfer to a small baking pan. Spoon a quarter of the oil plus the balsamic vinegar over the top of each onion and season with salt and pepper. Cover the dish with foil and bake 60 minutes, or until the center of the onions are tender when prodded with a skewer.

2. Meanwhile, make the stuffing. Coarsely grind the toasted almonds and sunflower seeds in a mini food processor. Tip them into a bowl and mix in the rest of the stuffing ingredients with the remaining oil, and season with salt and pepper.

3. Remove the onions from the oven. Take off the foil, carefully open up the onions slightly and divide the stuffing mixture among them, spooning it into the center of each one. Return them to the oven, uncovered, and roast another 15 minutes until the stuffing has heated through and is slightly crisp on top. Serve the onions on their slice of cooked bread with the rainbow chard on the side.

Like tofu, tempeh is made from soybeans, but it is fermented and has a nuttier, coarser texture. You can buy tempeh chilled, but I tend to buy it frozen in large blocks so I can simply slice off the amount needed.

Tempeh with Peanut Sauce

Serves: 4   **Preparation time:** 15 minutes, plus at least 1 hour marinating
Cooking time: 25 minutes

2 tablespoons dark soy sauce
1 tablespoon honey
1 tablespoon sunflower oil
1 tablespoon toasted sesame oil
7 ounces tempeh or tofu, drained, patted dry
    and cubed (about 1⅔ cups)
9 ounces medium egg noodles
chopped scallions and cilantro,
    to serve

PEANUT SAUCE
⅓ cup peanut butter
2 tablespoons rice wine vinegar
2 tablespoons dark soy sauce
2 tablespoons light brown sugar
1 tablespoon tahini paste
½ teaspoon dried red pepper flakes
1-inch piece of ginger root,
    peeled and chopped
1 teaspoon turmeric

1. Mix together the soy sauce, honey, sunflower oil and sesame oil in a shallow dish. Add the tempeh and turn to coat it in the marinade, then let marinate 1 hour, or until ready to use—the longer the better.

2. Meanwhile, make the peanut sauce. Blend together all the ingredients with ¼ cup hot water until smooth, then set to one side.

3. Preheat the oven to 350°F. Remove the tempeh from the marinade and spread it out on a large cookie sheet. Roast 25 minutes, turning once, until golden all over.

4. Meanwhile, cook the noodles following the package instructions. Drain, reserving a little of the cooking water. Return the noodles to the pot and stir in the peanut sauce, adding as much of the reserved cooking water as needed to make a slightly runny sauce. Serve the peanut noodles topped with the tempeh, sprinkled with scallions and cilantro.

Tahini is also used in the Tahini and Squash Dip (see page 90).

Make double the quantity of peanut sauce and freeze up to 3 months. Reheat from frozen with a splash of water, and use as a sauce, a dip or the base of a dressing.

This curry changes depending on what I have lying around in the kitchen. So you could also use a combination of red bell pepper, spinach and mushrooms, or root veg in the winter for a more substantial dish. Similarly, try making your own blends of spice mixes (see page 15); this one has a Sri Lankan feel and works well with coconut-based curries.

Sri Lankan Coconut Curry

Serves: *4* ***Preparation time:*** *15 minutes, plus making the spice mix*
Cooking time: *25 minutes*

1 large onion
4 garlic cloves
2-inch piece of ginger root, peeled and sliced
3 tablespoons sunflower oil
2½ tablespoons Curry Spice Mix (see page 15) or medium curry powder
1 x 14-ounce can coconut milk
3 tomatoes, seeded and chopped
1 teaspoon vegetable bouillon powder

1 cauliflower, cut into small florets
¾ cup fine green beans, cut into thirds
juice of 1 lime
1 teaspoon soft light brown sugar
3 handfuls of fresh cilantro leaves and stalks, chopped
sea salt and freshly ground black pepper
2 tablespoons toasted slivered almonds, to serve

1. Put the onion, garlic and ginger in a food processor and blend to a coarse paste. Heat the oil in a large, heavy pan over medium-low heat, add the onion paste and fry 5 minutes, stirring regularly, until softened.

2. Stir in 2 tablespoons of the spice mix, then add the coconut milk, tomatoes and 1 cup water and bring up to boiling point. Stir in the bouillon powder, turn the heat down slightly and simmer 5 minutes.

3. Add the cauliflower and green beans and cook, part-covered, 12 minutes until the vegetables are almost cooked. Stir in the lime juice, sugar, 2 handfuls of the cilantro and the remaining spice mix. Season well and cook, part-covered, another 3 minutes or until the vegetables are tender. Remove the lid if the sauce needs to thicken. Serve sprinkled with the almonds and the remaining cilantro.

Cans of coconut milk are often cheaper in Asian markets, or check out the "world food" section in grocery stores.

Wild sweet chestnuts are delicious in this autumnal pie, with its crisp suet crust. If you are roasting them, make sure you cut a small slit in the skin first or they may explode in the oven — believe me, I speak from experience!

Chestnut and Mushroom Pie

Serves: 4–6   **Preparation time:** 20 minutes, plus 30 minutes chilling
Cooking time: 1 hour

2 tablespoons sunflower oil
3 leeks, chopped
2 carrots, cubed (or you could use any leftover
    cooked root vegetables)
1 chestnut (or crimini) mushrooms, chopped
3 garlic cloves, finely chopped
7 ounces cooked peeled chestnuts, chopped
1 heaped tablespoon chopped sage leaves
1 heaped tablespoon thyme leaves or
    2 teaspoons dried thyme
1 heaped tablespoon all-purpose flour

⅞ cup light beer
⅞ cup Vegetable Stock (see page 14)
1 egg, lightly beaten
sea salt and freshly ground black pepper

SUET PASTRY DOUGH
1¾ cup plus 2 tablespoons all-purpose flour,
    plus extra for dusting
½ teaspoon baking powder
1 cup vegetable suet
½ teaspoon sea salt

1. Mix together the flour, baking powder, suet and salt in a large mixing bowl. Stir in ⅔ cup water and bring together to make a ball of dough. Wrap in plastic wrap and chill 30 minutes.

2. Meanwhile, make the pie filling. Heat the oil in a large, heavy pot over medium heat. Add the leeks and carrots, turn the heat down slightly and cook, part-covered, 6 minutes until the leeks are tender. Add the mushrooms and cook another 4 minutes until tender. Stir in the garlic, chestnuts and herbs, then add the flour and cook, stirring, 1 minute. Pour in the ale, stir, and gently boil, uncovered, 5 minutes or until reduced by half. Add the stock and cook, part-covered, 10 minutes. Remove the lid if the sauce is too thin. Season with salt and pepper.

3. Preheat the oven to 375°F. Tip the filling into a pie dish or casserole dish, about 11 inches square. Roll out the pastry dough on a lightly floured work surface until it's ¼ inch thick. Cut a long ½-inch strip of dough from the edge. Brush the rim of the pie dish with a little beaten egg, top with the pastry dough strip and brush with more egg. Top with the pastry dough lid, then press and crimp the edges. Brush the top with egg and prick the middle with a fork. Bake 30 minutes until cooked and golden.

You can gather *sweet chestnuts* in the fall. They're easier to harvest when they've dropped to the ground, but retrieve them early in the day before the squirrels get them! Cook the chestnuts in a pan of simmering water until the kernels are tender, then refresh in cold water and peel. Alternatively, roast them in the oven or cook in a special chestnut pan over a burner or open fire.

Sesame Seeds

Traditionally from Africa, slaves brought sesame seeds to America, yet these unassuming seeds are used in the cooking of a surprisingly diverse collection of countries located across the globe; their diminutive size does not appear to have held them back in any way. For example, in Europe sesame seeds are sprinkled over sweet and savory pastries and breads before baking, while in the Middle East they are ground into the thick, creamy paste known as tahini. In Japan, gomashio—made by grinding sesame seeds with salt—is a popular seasoning, and distinctive toasted sesame oil is often sprinkled over Far Eastern dishes at the end of cooking. The seeds, which come in red, black, yellow and the more usual creamy white, have a high oil content so are best kept in an airtight container in the refrigerator or freezer to stop them turning rancid.

The nutty flavor of sesame seeds is greatly enhanced by lightly toasting them in a dry skillet until they are just golden. Here, the seeds are combined with toasted flakes of nori seaweed and folded into sticky sushi rice to make Japanese-style patties, and then topped with some mustardy greens, thin strips of omelet and a sprinkling of peppery radish sprouts.

Sesame and Nori Cakes

Serves: 4   *Preparation time:* 15 minutes, plus 10 minutes standing
Cooking time: 25 minutes

2 cups sushi rice, rinsed 3 times
2 nori sheets
3 tablespoons sesame seeds
2 tablespoons butter
6 eggs
2 heaped tablespoons radish sprouts
sea salt and freshly ground black pepper

MUSTARD-SOY GREENS
1 dark green, leafy cabbage or
  4 bok choy, sliced
2 tablespoons prepared English mustard
¼ cup lemon juice
2 tablespoons light soy sauce

1. Put the rice in a pan, cover with 2¼ cups water and add 1 teaspoon salt. Bring to a boil, then cover with a lid, turn the heat down to its lowest setting and simmer 10 to 12 minutes until the water has been absorbed and the rice is tender and sticky. Remove from the heat and let stand 10 minutes, covered, until cooled slightly.

2. Meanwhile, heat a large, nonstick, dry skillet over medium heat. Toast the nori sheets, one at a time, 1½ minutes on each side, or until just crisp, then let cool. Add the sesame seeds to the pan and toast 2 minutes until just golden.

3. Add the sesame seeds to the pan of rice. Tear the nori sheets into small pieces and fold them into the rice in the pan with the sesame seeds, replace the lid and set to one side while you steam the cabbage greens 3 minutes until just tender. While the greens are cooking, mix together the mustard, lemon juice, soy sauce and 2 tablespoons water. Tip the cooked greens into a bowl, pour the mustard dressing over them and turn until coated.

4. To make the omelets, melt half the butter in the skillet over medium heat. Lightly beat 3 of the eggs in a bowl, season with salt and pepper and pour into the skillet. Turn the heat down slightly and swirl the pan so the egg covers the bottom of the pan and cook until just firm. Roll up the omelet, tip it onto a plate and repeat to make a second one. Cut each omelet into thin strips crosswise. With wet hands, form the sushi rice mixture into 4 round patties. Spoon the dressed greens on top in a pile and top with the omelet strips and radish sprouts.

Pictured on page 107.

Dukka

This Egyptian mixture of toasted nuts, seeds and spices is addictive. Toast **3 tablespoons coriander seeds**, **1 tablespoon cumin seeds** and **3 tablespoons each of sesame seeds**, **sunflower seeds** and **pumpkin seeds** in a large, dry skillet 2 to 3 minutes, shaking the pan occasionally until they smell toasted and are lightly colored. Remove from the pan and let cool. Toast a heaped **⅓ cup blanched almonds** and **¼ cup hazelnuts** in the same pan 5 minutes, then let cool. Tip the toasted nuts, seeds and spices into a mini grinder and grind to a coarse crumbly mixture. Transfer to a bowl, stir in **½ teaspoon dried red pepper flakes** and season well with **salt** and **pepper**.

Tamari Nuts and Seeds

Great for snacking on or sprinkled over stir-fries and rice dishes, tamari-coated nuts and seeds don't take long to make. Preheat the oven to 325°F. Put **2 handfuls of mixed nuts**, such as almonds, cashews and peanuts, in a bowl. Add **2 handfuls of mixed seeds**, including sesame, sunflower and pumpkin, then stir in **2 to 3 tablespoons tamari** or **soy sauce** until everything is coated. Tip onto a large cookie sheet (or you may need two) and spread out in an even layer. Roast 10 to 12 minutes, turning regularly, until they smell toasted. Keep an eye on them, as they burn easily. Tip into a bowl, let cool and store in an airtight container.

Sesame, Orange and Dandelion Salad

Toast **2 tablespoons sesame seeds** in a dry skillet until light golden. Wash **2 handfuls of young dandelion leaves**, drain well and put on a serving plate with **2 handfuls of watercress**. Slice **1 peeled orange** into rounds and put them on top of the salad greens. Mix together **2 tablespoons extra virgin olive oil** with **1 teaspoon honey** and **1 tablespoon lemon juice**, season with **salt** and **pepper** and spoon the dressing over the salad.

Chapter 5
Carton of Eggs

The perfect complete, nutritious food encased in a convenient,
individual package, the egg is a marvel of versatility and
for very little expense. Whether scrambled, boiled, fried,
poached or baked, used to thicken sauces, to bind fritters or to
add a golden glaze to pie crusts, eggs are a must in my kitchen.
Look out for Twice-Baked Cheese Soufflés, Easter Egg Pies,
Tunisian Eggs with Herb Yogurt and last, but by no means
least, a Rainbow Chard and Parmesan Tortino in this chapter.

This is based on the iconic Greek soup avgolemono, but is made with vegetable stock and added zucchini to form a light first course or a summery lunch. You could make it more substantial by upping the vegetables, perhaps including asparagus tips, fresh peas or fava beans when they are in season. I've used vermicelli noodles, but you could also try orzo, rice or even thin egg noodles.

Greek Egg and Lemon Soup

Serves: 4   *Preparation time:* 10 minutes, plus making the stock
Cooking time: 3 minutes

5 cups Vegetable Stock (see page 14)
4 ounces dried vermicelli noodles
1 large or 2 small zucchini, cubed
juice and finely grated zest of 1 lemon

2 teaspoons cornstarch
2 large eggs
sea salt and freshly ground black pepper
fennel fronds, to serve

1. Bring the stock to a boil in a large pot. Add the vermicelli and zucchini and cook 3 minutes until both are tender. Season with salt and pepper.

2. Meanwhile, put the lemon juice and zest in a mixing bowl and stir in the cornstarch until dissolved, then whisk in the eggs until combined.

3. Remove the pot from the heat. Add a spoonful of the hot stock to the egg mixture and whisk until combined. Pour the egg mixture into the pot, stirring continuously 2 minutes until the soup thickens slightly. Serve sprinkled with wild fennel fronds and seasoned with extra pepper.

Put an egg in a bowl of cold water — if it sinks horizontally, it's very fresh. If it tips up slightly, it could be up to 2 weeks old. If it floats, throw it away.

The fronds of *wild fennel* are prolific throughout the summer months, especially on wasteground and coastal areas. Like cultivated Florence fennel, the fronds have a sweet anise flavor, but the wild variety doesn't produce a bulb. Use the fronds as a flavorful herb and the thin stems sliced into salads. Clusters of yellow flowers produce seeds that can be harvested and dried in fall.

Scallions

are easy to grow from seed in pots in a sunny spot or in fertilized soil with good drainage. They are quick-growing; sow regularly from spring to late summer to ensure a steady supply. I'm also a fan of milder red scallions. Thin out young shoots to prevent overcrowding, and use in salads in the same way as chives or use in salads, stir-fries, pilafs, tortillas or stirred into mashed potatoes.

This Mexican dish is a great way of using up slightly stale tortillas (which in my house have a tendency to linger in the back of the bread bin). I can't claim that my version of this classic dish is authentic, as I mix the tomato salsa into the scrambled eggs rather than into the tortillas, and then serve the scramble on top of the crisp, fried tortillas, yet it still goes down well with the family.

Chilaquiles

Serves: *4*   **Preparation time:** *15 minutes*   **Cooking time:** *17 minutes*

6 corn tortillas
sunflower oil, for frying
4 vine-ripened tomatoes, seeded and chopped
6 scallions, thinly sliced
1 red chili, seeded and chopped
1 large handful of cilantro leaves, chopped
2 tablespoons butter

10 eggs, lightly beaten
good splash of chili sauce
sea salt and freshly ground black pepper

TO SERVE
bottled jalapeños, chopped
feta or other soft cheese, crumbled

1. Stack the tortillas on top of one another and cut them into 12 wedges. Pour a good layer of oil into a large skillet and heat over medium heat. Fry the tortilla wedges in four batches about 1 minute on each side until light golden and crisp, then drain on paper towels and set to one side.

2. Mix together the tomatoes, scallions, chili and half the cilantro. Pour all but 1 tablespoon of the oil out of the pan, turn the heat down to medium-low and add the butter. When the butter has melted, add the tomato salsa and cook, stirring, 3 minutes until softened.

3. Season the eggs with salt and pepper and stir in the chili sauce. Add to the pan and cook the eggs over low heat, turning the mixture gently until everything is combined and scrambled to a soft but cooked consistency.

4. Divide the tortilla wedges onto four serving plates and top with the scrambled egg mixture and the remaining cilantro. Scatter the jalapeños and feta over them before serving.

You can't beat the flavor of tomatoes ripened on the vine, but if you're faced with hard tomatoes, store them in a paper bag with a ripe banana or an apple to encourage ripening; the same technique works with avocados, too.

This is a great throw-together dish, made predominantly from staple ingredients. There are many North African variations of Tunisian Eggs, which are all based on the same idea but vary slightly in their use of spicing and choice of herbs. I also like to crumble Homemade Paneer (see page 17) or other soft, crumbly cheese over the top just before serving.

Tunisian Eggs with Herb Yogurt

Serves: 4   **Preparation time:** 15 minutes   **Cooking time:** 30 minutes

3 tablespoons olive oil
1 large onion, finely chopped
3 garlic cloves, finely chopped
1 large red bell pepper, seeded and chopped
2 teaspoons ground coriander
1 teaspoon ground cumin
1 teaspoon hot smoked paprika
½ teaspoon dried red pepper flakes
2 teaspoons thyme leaves or 1 teaspoon
   dried thyme
14-ounce can chopped tomatoes
1 teaspoon light brown sugar
4 large eggs

sea salt and freshly ground black pepper
crusty bread, to serve

HERB YOGURT
⅔ cup Wholemilk Yogurt (see page 16)
   or Greek yogurt
1 garlic clove, crushed
heaped ¼ cup chopped cilantro leaves
2 tablespoons chopped mint leaves, plus extra
   to serve
1 small handful of toasted chopped walnuts
¼ teaspoon sumac (optional)

1. Heat the oil in a large, deep skillet over medium heat. Add the onion and fry 6 minutes until softened but not colored. Add the garlic and red bell pepper and cook another 3 minutes, turning the heat down slightly if things start to brown. Stir in the spices and thyme followed by the tomatoes and sugar, then bring to a boil.

2. Turn the heat down to low and simmer, part-covered, 10 minutes until reduced and thickened. Season with salt and pepper and make four evenly spaced dips in the sauce. Crack the eggs into the dips, cover with a lid and cook gently 8 minutes, or until the egg whites are set but the yolks are still a little runny.

3. While the eggs are cooking, mix together the yogurt, garlic, cilantro and mint in a bowl. Season with salt and pepper and scatter in the walnuts and sumac, if using. Sprinkle the eggs with extra mint and serve with the herb yogurt and crusty bread.

Preparing baked eggs is pretty straightforward, and quantities can readily be increased or decreased depending on how many you're feeding. This version is topped with a curry-spiced cream and gives a simple twist on the classic eggs Florentine with spinach, cream and a sprinkling of cheese. I've made the most of some foraged wild field mushrooms, though you could also use puffballs or, if you're lucky enough to find them, cèpes (porcini).

Spiced Baked Eggs

Serves: 4   *Preparation time:* 10 minutes   *Cooking time:* 25 minutes

2 tablespoons butter, plus extra for greasing
2 teaspoons olive oil
9 ounces field mushrooms or mushrooms of choice, finely chopped
5 large handfuls of Swiss chard, tough stalks removed, leaves shredded

4 large eggs
½ cup heavy cream
1 tablespoon mild curry powder
sea salt and freshly ground black pepper
toasted bread, to serve

1. Preheat the oven to 375°F and lightly butter four deep ramekin dishes. Heat the butter and oil in a large skillet over medium heat. Add the mushrooms and fry 4 minutes until any liquid has evaporated and they start to turn crisp. Add the chard and cook another 3 to 4 minutes until wilted and tender.

2. Divide the mushroom mixture into the prepared ramekins, then crack an egg into each one. Mix together the cream and curry powder, season with salt and pepper and spoon over it the eggs so they are completely covered.

3. Put the ramekins in a deep baking pan to make your "water bath." Pour into the pan enough just-boiled water to come three quarters of the way up the sides. This will help the eggs to cook evenly. Carefully transfer the pan to the oven and cook 16 to 18 minutes until the whites of the eggs are just set but the yolks remain runny (you can cook them slightly longer if you prefer a set egg). Season with more pepper and serve with toasted bread.

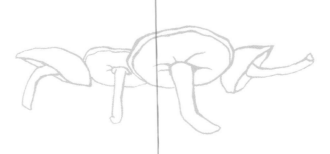

This is a hybrid of my children's two favorite things—pizza and frittata—and makes a simple midweek meal when served with a mixed salad. Feel free to add your own favorite toppings or whatever you have at hand; this is a great way to use up leftover cheese, vegetables, olives, capers or anything else you choose. You need a heavy 9-inch nonstick pan with an ovenproof handle.

Pizzata

Serves: 4   **Preparation time:** 15 minutes   **Cooking time:** 20 minutes

3 boiling potatoes, peeled and quartered
2 tablespoons olive oil
1 large onion, chopped
4 sundried tomatoes, chopped
8 eggs, lightly beaten
4½ ounces drained mozzarella cheese,
   patted dry and torn into pieces

1 long red chili, seeded and chopped
   (optional)
2 tablespoons basil pesto
1 handful of small basil leaves
sea salt and freshly ground black pepper

1. Cook the potatoes in boiling salted water 10 minutes, or until tender. Drain and let cool slightly, then cube them.

2. Meanwhile, heat the oil in a large, deep, nonstick ovenproof skillet over medium heat. Add the onion and fry 8 minutes until softened but not colored. Stir in the cooked potatoes and sundried tomatoes and spread them over the bottom of the pan in an even layer.

3. Preheat the broiler to medium. Season the eggs with salt and pepper, then pour them into the pan over the onion mixture. Turn the burner down to medium-low and cook the eggs gently, without stirring, 8 minutes, or until the bottom is set and light golden. Scatter the mozzarella and chili, if using, over the top and dot with spoonfuls of the pesto. Broil 2 to 3 minutes until the mozzarella has just melted. Serve sprinkled with the basil and cut into wedges.

Sundried tomatoes are also used in Pumpkin Seed Rolls (see page 97).

If your skillet has lost its nonstick coating, you can temper it for a new lease of life. First add a little oil and rub it all over the skillet with a paper towel. Heat the skillet over high heat until the oil starts to smoke, then remove the skillet from the heat. Using a large crumpled paper towel, wipe the bottom of the skillet, taking care not to burn yourself. Let the skillet cool, and it is ready to use.

These are based on the Greek Easter pie, which is filled with foraged wild greens, and traditionally celebrates the arrival of spring. For a change, I've hidden an egg in the center of each pie. You could use a deep muffin pan for the pies instead of steamed-pudding molds.

Easter Egg Pies

Serves: 4   *Preparation time:* 20 minutes   *Cooking time:* 55 minutes

¼ cup (½ stick) butter, melted
5 small eggs
2 tablespoons olive oil
1 large onion, finely chopped
2 garlic cloves, finely chopped
9 ounces greens, such as nettles, arugula and
  chard, stalks removed, leaves shredded

2 cups farmer cheese (or other curd cheese)
4 teaspoons thyme leaves or 2 teaspoons
  dried thyme
½ teaspoon freshly grated nutmeg
8 sheets of phyllo pastry, 9 × 14 inches
sea salt and freshly ground black pepper

1. Preheat the oven to 375°F and brush four deep metal steamed-pudding molds (about 1 cup each) with some of the melted butter. Hard-boil 4 of the eggs, then refresh under cold running water, peel and set to one side. Meanwhile, heat the oil in a large skillet over medium heat. Add the onion and fry 8 minutes until softened and starting to color. Stir in the garlic and cook another 2 minutes, stirring regularly.

2. If using nettles, wash them well and cook in a pot with no extra water 4 minutes to neutralize the sting. Drain well, pat dry and tip into a large bowl along with the onion mixture. Stir in the remaining mixed greens, curd cheese, thyme and nutmeg. Lightly beat the remaining egg and add to the bowl, season well with salt and pepper and stir until combined.

3. Lay out 1 sheet of the phyllo dough, brush half with butter and fold in half to cover the butter-coated part. Carefully press the phyllo sheet into one of the prepared molds, leaving the excess phyllo overhanging. Repeat with a second phyllo sheet, then place it across the first sheet and press it into the bottom to make a pastry shell, again leaving an overhang.

4. Put a large tablespoonful of the greens mixture in the bottom of the phyllo-lined mold and put a peeled hard-boiled egg upright in it. Spoon the greens mixture around and on top of the egg, pressing down with your fingers and filling the mold to the brim. Brush the overhanging pastry with more melted butter and fold it over the filling, scrunching to seal the top. Brush with more butter, then repeat to make 4 pies. Put the pies on a baking sheet and bake 30 to 40 minutes until golden and crisp. Let cool slightly in the molds, then carefully turn them out. If the pastry shells are a little soft, return the pies to the oven another 5 minutes to crisp up.

Forage for _nettles_ in spring, when the leaves are young and tender. Wearing thick gloves and using scissors, gather the youngest leaves and, as the season progresses, only pick the tips—the older leaves can be bitter. Gather nettles away from roads, wash well before cooking and enjoy this herby, nutritious leaf—a good source of iron, vitamins A and C and a surprisingly generous amount of protein.

If you've always shied away from making soufflés, I've found these fail-proof. They can be made the day before and reheated briefly before serving; they magically rise up when baked for the second time.

Twice-Baked Cheese Soufflés

Serves: *4*   **Preparation time:** *15 minutes, plus 30 minutes infusing*
Cooking time: *50 minutes*

1 cup milk minus 2 tablespoons
1 bay leaf
1 large garlic clove, cut in half
3½ tablespoons butter
⅓ cup all-purpose flour
2 teaspoons Dijon mustard

1½ cups grated sharp cheddar cheese
2 tablespoons chopped chives, plus extra
  to serve
3 eggs, separated
¼ cup heavy cream
crisp green salad, to serve

1. Heat the milk in a small pan with the bay leaf and garlic until warm, then turn off the heat and let infuse 30 minutes. Remove the bay leaf and garlic from the milk and reheat until warm. Meanwhile, preheat the oven to 400°F and heat a large cookie sheet.

2. Melt the butter in a medium pan and use a little to grease four deep 1-cup ramekins. Whisk the flour into the remaining melted butter over medium heat and cook, stirring, 1 minute to make a "roux."

3. Gradually stir the warm milk into the roux to make your soufflé mixture. Bring to a boil, then turn the heat down to low and simmer 5 minutes, stirring, until thick and smooth. Pour the soufflé mixture into a bowl and stir in the mustard, cheddar and chives. Beat in the egg yolks, one at a time.

4. In a separate large bowl, beat the egg whites with a clean beater until they form stiff peaks. Using a metal spoon, fold the egg whites into the cheese mixture in two batches, then spoon it into the prepared ramekins. Put the ramekins on the heated cookie sheet and bake 18 to 20 minutes until risen. Let cool, run a knife around the edge of the soufflés and turn them out. Chill until ready to serve.

5. Just before serving, heat the oven to 425°F. Put the soufflés on a cookie sheet, then spoon 1 tablespoon of the cream over each one. Bake 10 to 12 minutes until risen. Sprinkle the soufflés with the chives and serve with a green salad.

This has a Scandi feel, with the crisp, golden latkes (potato pancakes) topped with soft-boiled eggs and a mustard sour cream sauce. A sprinkling of wild fennel fronds adds the finishing touch. Freeze any leftover cooked and cooled latkes on a cookie sheet in the freezer, then transfer to a ziploc bag. Reheat from frozen in the oven until crisp and heated through.

Potato and Parsnip Latkes with Wild Fennel

Serves: 4   *Preparation time:* 20 minutes   *Cooking time:* 20 minutes

2 white potatoes, about 1¼ pounds
2 parsnips, about 10½ ounces
⅓ cup all-purpose flour
1 teaspoon baking powder
1 tablespoon fennel or caraway seeds
1 teaspoon sea salt
¼ teaspoon coarsely ground black pepper
2 eggs, lightly beaten
sunflower oil, for shallow-frying

TO SERVE
6 large eggs
½ cup sour cream
2 teaspoons prepared English mustard
3 cooked beets, cubed
a few wild fennel fronds (see page 113)

1. Coarsely grate the potatoes and parsnips using a box grater or a food processor; you want long, thin strands. Transfer half the vegetables to a clean lintfree dish towel and wring out as much liquid as possible, then repeat with the remaining vegetables. Put in a bowl and stir in the flour, baking powder, fennel seeds, and salt and pepper until combined. Add the beaten eggs and stir again.

2. Preheat the oven to 150°F. Heat enough oil to cover the bottom of a large, nonstick skillet over medium heat. Take a small handful of the vegetable mixture, letting the eggy batter drain off a little, and put it into the pan. Flatten slightly with a spatula into a rough-edged 3½-inch patty, then repeat so you have 3 latkes in the pan, and fry 3 minutes on each side until golden and crisp. Transfer the latkes to a paper towel-lined baking sheet and keep warm in the oven while you cook the remaining latkes. The mixture will make 8 in total.

3. Put the eggs in a saucepan and cover with cold water. Bring to a boil and boil gently 5 minutes until soft-boiled. Meanwhile, mix together the sour cream and mustard in a bowl.

4. Peel the eggs and cut in half lengthwise. Put the latkes on four plates and top each serving with 3 egg halves. Drizzle the mustard sour cream over them and spoon the beets by the side. Season with salt and pepper and serve sprinkled with fennel fronds.

Samphire (salicornia) can be expensive, so it's worth foraging for. There are two types: *marsh samphire* (glasswort), which grows on shorelines and salt marshes, and *rock samphire* which, unsurprisingly, likes rocky areas. Both have a wonderful crisp texture and saltiness reminiscent of the sea and are best picked young in early summer. Eat raw in salads, steam lightly or briefly sauté in butter.

Poaching eggs can be tricky, but if you follow the instructions below you should get good results. This recipe makes an elegant weekend meal when served with Asian-Style Mash (see page 22) and samphire (salicornia).

Eggs with Lemongrass Cream

Serves: *4* ***Preparation time:*** *15 minutes, plus making the stock and 30 minutes infusing* ***Cooking time:*** *25 minutes*

8 eggs
1 teaspoon white wine vinegar
sea salt and freshly ground black pepper

TO SERVE
1 recipe quantity Asian-Style Mash
  (see page 22)
2 tablespoons chopped chives
1 red chili, seeded and chopped
samphire or green beans

LEMONGRASS CREAM SAUCE
2 long lemongrass stalks, bruised
1 cup Vegetable Stock (see page 14)
scant ½ cup creamy top from a can of
  coconut milk
2 teaspoons cornstarch, mixed with a
  little water
finely grated zest of 1 large lime and
  juice of ½ lime

1. For the sauce, put the lemongrass and stock in a small pan and bring to a boil; boil 10 minutes until reduced by a third. Remove from the heat and let infuse 30 minutes. Return the pan to the heat, stir in the coconut milk and the cornstarch mixture and return to a boil, stirring continuously. Turn the heat down and simmer 8 to 10 minutes until reduced and thickened to a creamy consistency. Add the lime zest and juice, season with salt and pepper and gently heat through, stirring. Set to one side.

2. To poach the eggs, fill a large, deep skillet with just-boiled water from the kettle, at least 2 inches deep. When the water starts to simmer, turn the heat down to medium-low and add the vinegar. Crack the eggs one at a time into a cup and carefully slip them into the gently simmering water (you may need to cook them in two batches—if so, reheat very briefly in hot water just before you serve them). Poach the eggs 2 to 3 minutes until the whites are set but the yolks remain runny.

3. Remove the lemongrass from the sauce and reheat, if necessary. Divide the Asian-Style Mash onto four plates. Lift the eggs out of the water with a slotted spoon and put on top of the mash, spoon the sauce over them and around the edge and sprinkle with chives and chili. Season with salt and pepper and serve with samphire.

👉 Omelet

An omelet is the ultimate frugal dish: the way it's possible to transform a couple of eggs, a pinch of salt and a tablespoon of butter into a delicious meal is truly satisfying. Fantastic plain, an omelet is also the perfect vehicle for flavorings and fillings—sweet or savory. A sprinkling of fresh herbs, a filling of grated cheese or sautéed vegetables is all you need. Also try making a thin, one-egg omelet (add 1 teaspoon water), slicing it into narrow strips and serving it on top of Oriental soups, rice and noodle dishes. Then there are the flat, open-faced omelets such as the Italian frittata, Spanish tortilla or the Middle Eastern eggah, which are made with a large proportion of filling ingredients added to the egg, cooked gently on the stove and finished under the broiler or in the oven. As with all egg dishes, it's important not to overcook omelets. It's also essential to cook them in a heavy, nonstick pan.

▶▶

A tortino is an oven-baked version of the Italian frittata, and makes a simple meal or the perfect picnic dish. This tortino has a slightly autumnal flavor with the rich earthiness of dried porcini and leafy greens; you can alter the flavorings to suit the season. A summery alternative might include strips of red bell pepper, cubed zucchini and chopped spinach. Whatever you choose, be generous with the ratio of filling to egg.

Rainbow Chard and Parmesan Tortino

Serves: 4   **Preparation time:** 15 minutes, plus 20 minutes soaking and 10 minutes resting   **Cooking time:** 45 minutes

1 ounce dried porcini (cèpes)
2 tablespoons olive oil
1 large onion, finely chopped
3 garlic cloves, finely chopped
9½ ounces rainbow chard, leaves stripped away from the stalks, thick stalks and stems removed, thin stalks finely sliced
butter, for greasing

2 teaspoons thyme leaves or 1 teaspoon dried thyme
1 cup vegetarian parmesan cheese, finely grated
7 eggs, lightly beaten
⅓ cup day-old breadcrumbs
sea salt and freshly ground black pepper

1. Cover the porcini in just-boiled water and let soften 20 minutes, then drain, reserving the soaking liquor for another recipe. Squeeze out any remaining water and roughly chop the porcini.

2. Meanwhile, heat the oil in a large, nonstick skillet over medium heat. Add the onion and fry 5 minutes until softened. Add the garlic and sliced chard stalks and cook another 3 minutes, then tip in the porcini and cook another 5 minutes, followed by the thyme.

3. Preheat the oven to 350°F. Generously butter an 8-inch springform cake pan and line the bottom with baking parchment. Shred the chard leaves and put them in a large mixing bowl along with the onion mixture. Add the parmesan, reserving 2 tablespoons, and the eggs. Season well with salt and pepper and stir until combined.

4. Sprinkle half the breadcrumbs in an even layer into the bottom of the pan. Pour the egg mixture into the pan, so everything is evenly distributed, and sprinkle with the remaining breadcrumbs and the reserved parmesan. Bake 35 to 40 minutes until set. Let the tortino rest in the pan 10 minutes before removing it. Serve cut into wedges.

Pictured on page 127.

Eggah

Eggah is a Middle Eastern version of a Spanish tortilla or Italian frittata. Sauté **1 large cubed zucchini** in **2 teaspoons olive oil** in a large, nonstick, heavy, ovenproof skillet 5 minutes until softened and slightly colored. Tip into a large bowl along with **2½ cups chopped baby spinach leaves**, **2 cups chopped scallions**, **2 handfuls of chopped cilantro**, **1 teaspoon allspice** and **½ teaspoon cumin seeds**. Beat **8 large eggs** and season well with **salt** and **pepper**. Pour the egg mixture over the spinach mixture and stir until combined. Heat **2 teaspoons olive oil** in the skillet over medium-low heat. Pour in the egg mixture and cook 10 minutes until the bottom is light golden and set. Preheat the broiler to medium and put the skillet under the broiler 3 minutes, or until set. Serve cut into wedges.

Sous-Vide Omelet

This is my home-style version of sous-vide (the method of cooking food in a vacuum-sealed bag in a water bath), which doesn't require any special equipment. It's an interesting concept and produces an omelet with a soft, creamy consistency. For two people, pour just-boiled water into a large, deep sauté pan until nearly full and set over low heat—the water should be just simmering. Whisk together **4 eggs** with **1 tablespoon light cream** and add **1 tablespoon chopped chives** and season with **salt** and **pepper**. Pour the mixture into a ziploc freezer bag, squeeze out as much air as possible and seal. Fold the top of the bag over a couple of times to make a small rectangular package. Put the package in the water and press down with a spatula until submerged, cover and simmer the eggs 8 to 10 minutes until the omelet is just set. Carefully remove the bag from the water and let the omelet settle in the bottom of the bag. Gently slide the omelet onto serving plates.

Sushi Rolls

Use a thin, **one-egg omelet** to encase rice and/or vegetable rolls instead of using nori sheets. Trim the omelet to make a square and arrange stir-fried **scallions**, **red bell pepper** and **asparagus** down the middle. Roll up the omelet and cut into 1-inch lengths, stand the rolls up on their end and serve with **soy sauce** and **pickled ginger**.

Chapter 6
Slice of Cheese (and Other Dairy)

For the home cook, dairy products are incredibly varied and add a wonderful flavor and texture to all manner of dishes. Cheeses that are made from milk from cows, ewes, goats or even buffalo will all have individual characteristics depending on where they're from, how they're produced and the way they're aged. The recipes in this chapter encapsulate this versatility, such as the creamy yet potent Potted Cheese with Elderflower Pears, fresh and light Ricotta and Wild Greens Dumplings and nutty-tasting Beet Top, Scallion and Gruyère Tart.

This smooth pâté makes use of any leftover or tail-end bits of cheese you might have in the refrigerator. You can use a single type of goat, cow or sheep cheese, or try a combination: a piquant blue; a crumbly, aged hard cheese; or a soft, creamy one are all possibilities, but look for a balance of flavors. I wanted to make use of the short elderflower season by poaching the pears in an elderflower-infused syrup. The result is delicately perfumed, succulent fruit that complements the creamy tanginess of the potted cheese.

Potted Cheese with Elderflower Pears

Serves: *4*   **Preparation time:** *15 minutes, plus making the syrup and chilling*
Cooking time: *20 minutes*

1 cup Elderflower Syrup (see page 25)
  or cordial
4 just-ripe but not mushy pears, peeled
  and cut in half lengthwise
light rye bread, toasted, to serve

POTTED CHEESE
⅓ cup plus 2 teaspoons (¾ stick)
  very soft butter
4½ ounces Dolcelatte, cut into small pieces
heaped ½ cup vegetarian parmesan
  cheese, grated
2 tablespoons semi-dry flowery white wine
  or sherry
freshly ground black pepper

1. Put the elderflower syrup in a saucepan with 1¼ cups water. Add the pears—they should be just covered by the liquid, and if necessary add a little more water, but you don't want the syrup to be too diluted. Bring to a gentle boil, then turn the heat down and simmer, part-covered, 15 to 20 minutes until the pears are tender. Remove from the heat and let the pears cool in the syrup.

2. Meanwhile, put the butter, cheese and wine in a mixing bowl, and beat with a wooden spoon until combined. Season with pepper, and spoon the mixture into four small ramekins. Smooth the top and chill until firm. Remove the potted cheese from the refrigerator 20 minutes before serving to soften, and serve with the poached pears and toast.

Elderflowers

grow profusely but have a
relatively short season, so make the
most of the delicately perfumed
clusters of creamy-white flowers in early
to mid-summer (see page 25). Early fall
welcomes the elderberry with its distinctive
heads of small, deep purple berries.
The berries have to be cooked and
make a delicious syrup, pie filling
mixed with other seasonal
fruit, or jam.

There's a knack to opening a fresh coconut, and it requires a steady hand. Carefully bore two holes through the "eyes" in the top with a screwdriver or drill, and drain the liquid (it makes a super-hydrating drink). Using a wooden mallet or the blunt side of a heavy blade, firmly strike the coconut around its equator until it splits in half, then cut the coconut meat from the outer shell and brown skin.

Tandoori Halloumi with Coconut and Pineapple Salad

Serves: 4 *Preparation time:* 15 minutes *Cooking time:* 5 minutes

3 tablespoons tandoori spice mix
11½ ounces halloumi, rinsed, patted dry and sliced lengthwise into 8 thick slices
½ pineapple, skin removed, cored and cut into bite-size pieces
2 cups drained canned chickpeas or cooked dried chickpeas (see pages 8–9)

1 to 2 long green chilies, seeded and chopped
1 small red onion, chopped
¾ cup fresh coconut, coarsely grated
2 handfuls of cilantro leaves, chopped
juice of 1½ to 2 limes
1 tablespoon sunflower oil
sea salt and freshly ground black pepper

1. Sprinkle the spice mix over a plate and season with pepper. Coat both sides of each halloumi slice in the spices and set to one side.

2. Put the pineapple, chickpeas, green chilies, red onion, fresh coconut and cilantro in a serving bowl. Squeeze over then the smaller quantity of lime juice, and season with salt and pepper. Toss until everything is combined, then taste, adding more lime juice and/or seasoning if needed.

3. Heat the oil in a large, nonstick skillet over medium heat. Cook the halloumi 3 to 4 minutes, turning once, until softened and slightly colored. Serve immediately with the salad.

An alternative way to open a coconut is to freeze it overnight. The next day, crack the shell as above and the flesh should come away more easily from the shell and brown skin.

This is a great summer salad with a lively combination of flavors: cooling, sweet watermelon; tangy lime juice; and slight heat from the fresh chili — all counterbalanced by the salty sharpness of the feta cheese. Homemade Paneer (see page 17) works well instead of the feta, too.

Watermelon, Feta and Mint Salad

Serves: 4   Preparation time: 15 minutes

1¼ pounds watermelon, seeds removed if
  you like, cut into ¾-inch cubes
1 small red onion, thinly sliced into rings
20 pitted black olives
4½ ounces sheep feta cheese or Homemade
  Paneer (see page 17), cubed
1 small handful of mint leaves

1 long red chili, seeded and thinly sliced
  into rings
juice and pared rind of 1 small lime, cut into
  very fine strips
2 to 3 tablespoons extra virgin olive oil
sea salt and freshly ground black pepper
warm flatbreads, to serve

1. Put the cubed watermelon on a large serving plate and scatter the red onion, olives, feta, mint and chili over the top.

2. Drizzle the lime juice over the salad and sprinkle with the strips of lime rind. Drizzle with the olive oil, to taste, and season with salt and pepper. Serve at room temperature with warm flatbreads.

Extend the life of fresh chilies by storing them in an airtight container in the freezer. Defrost briefly to make them easier to slice before using in a recipe.

Mint

is a versatile addition to a kitchen garden, but it's also a vigorous herb that needs containing, otherwise it can become too prolific. Grow it in pots, or alternatively plant the pot it comes in—making sure it allows enough room for growth—right into the earth. There are many varieties of mint and it's worth checking out some of the more unusual ones, such as chocolate or apple!

Try to use a crumbly goat cheese rather than a soft, runny one to make these thick, savory pancakes. They are good eaten simply—for example, spread with garlic butter or with a herb-infused yogurt—but also make a more substantial meal when served with Pomegranate Salsa (see page 21).

Goat Cheese Pancakes

Serves: 4   **Preparation time:** 20 minutes   **Cooking time:** 1 hour

1 cup plus 2 tablespoons self-rising flour
1 teaspoon baking powder
½ teaspoon sea salt
3 eggs, separated
⅔ cup milk
3½ tablespoons butter, melted
3½ ounces rindless goat cheese, crumbled

3 handfuls of baby spinach or young sea beet
   leaves, finely chopped
5 scallions, finely sliced
3 tablespoons chopped cilantro leaves
sunflower oil, for frying
freshly ground black pepper
Pomegranate Salsa (see page 21), to serve

1. Mix together the flour, baking powder and salt in a large mixing bowl. Using a balloon whisk, mix in the egg yolks, milk and melted butter, then stir in the goat cheese, spinach, scallions and cilantro. Season with pepper.

2. Beat the egg whites to soft peaks and gently fold them into the goat cheese batter.

3. Pour a little oil into a large, non-stick, heavy skillet and place over medium heat. For each pancake, ladle in 3 tablespoons of batter and cook 4 to 5 minutes, turning once, until golden. Drain on paper towels and keep warm in a low oven. Repeat, adding more oil to the pan as needed until the batter is used up; it should make about 12 pancakes. Serve with the Pomegranate Salsa.

If a recipe calls for just the green part of scallions, don't ditch the white parts—regrow them. Stand them in a glass with about 2 inches water. Put in a light place and watch the green parts sprout, topping up the glass with more water when necessary. After about 5 days the green parts will be ready to cut and use again—you can do this a couple of times before the scallion runs out of momentum.

To me, curries often taste better the day after making, and this spicy lentil—tomato sauce is no exception. A day allows the spices time to get to know each other; to mingle and meld. Serve with a scattering of crumbled Homemade Paneer (see page 17), Mango Chutney (see page 19) and warmed nan bread. A handful of Crispy Onions and Ginger (see page 23) would be good, too.

Lentil Sambar with Paneer

Serves: 4   *Preparation time:* 15 minutes   *Cooking time:* 55 minutes

½ cup dried split red lentils, rinsed
7 garlic cloves, peeled
1 ounce root ginger, peeled and chopped
1 red chili
⅓ cup canola or vegetable oil
2 onions, chopped
2 tablespoons Curry Spice Mix (see page 15)
5 vine-ripened tomatoes, roughly chopped
2 teaspoons brown sugar
½ teaspoon dried red pepper flakes (optional)

2 tablespoons tamarind paste or lemon juice
sea salt and freshly ground black pepper

TO SERVE
½ recipe quantity Homemade Paneer
  (see page 17), crumbled
3 tablespoons chopped cilantro leaves
Crispy Onions and Ginger (see page 23),
  optional
Mango Chutney (see page 19), optional

1. Put the lentils in a pan and cover generously with water. Bring to a boil, then turn the heat down and simmer, part-covered, 15 minutes until tender. Drain and set to one side.

2. Blend the garlic, ginger and red chili with ¼ cup water until smooth. Set to one side.

3. Heat the oil in a pot over medium heat. Add the onions and cook 15 minutes, stirring occasionally, until just beginning to color. Add the spice mix and the garlic paste and cook another 5 minutes, stirring regularly.

4. Stir in the tomatoes, sugar, red pepper flakes, if using, tamarind, cooked lentils and ½ cup water, and bring to a boil. Turn the heat down slightly and simmer 15 minutes, part-covered, until reduced to a thick sauce. Season with salt and pepper and sprinkle with the paneer, cilantro and Crispy Onions and Ginger, if using. Serve with spoonfuls of mango chutney.

To freeze the sambar, omit the paneer and cilantro and freeze flat in ziploc bags. There's no need to defrost; add a splash of water and heat gently in a covered pan.

Wild greens are a good alternative to cultivated spinach. Opt for young leaves, which are less bitter; you can reduce bitterness by soaking them in salted water 30 minutes, then drain and rinse before cooking.

Ricotta and Wild Greens Dumplings

Serves: 4   *Preparation time:* 20 minutes   *Cooking time:* 30 minutes

1 tablespoon olive oil
2 heaped cups wild greens, such as Good
   King Henry, wild watercress, Alexanders or
   sea beet (or double the quantity of spinach),
   stems removed, leaves shredded
2 heaped cups baby spinach leaves, shredded
1 large egg, separated
9 ounces ricotta cheese, drained
⅔ cup vegetarian parmesan cheese, grated
½ cup all-purpose flour, plus extra for dusting

2 tablespoons chopped basil leaves,
   plus extra to serve
sea salt and freshly ground black pepper

TOMATO SAUCE
2 tablespoons olive oil
2 large garlic cloves, finely chopped
3 cups canned chopped tomatoes
3 large basil sprigs
1 tablespoon tomato paste
1 teaspoon sugar

1. To make the tomato sauce, put the oil and garlic in a large pot over medium-low heat and cook gently 1 minute until the garlic is softened but not colored. Add the tomatoes and basil sprigs and bring to a gentle boil, then turn the heat down, stir in the tomato paste and sugar, and simmer, part-covered, 10 minutes until reduced and thickened. Season with salt and pepper.

2. Meanwhile, make the dumplings. Heat the oil in a large, non-stick skillet over medium heat. Add the wild greens and spinach and sauté 3 minutes, stirring regularly, until wilted and tender. Mix the greens with the egg yolk, ricotta, parmesan, flour and basil, then season with salt and pepper. Beat the egg white with an electric beater until it forms stiff peaks, then fold it gently into the ricotta mixture.

3. Bring a large pot of salted water to a boil. Using floured hands, make small balls about the size of a large walnut with the ricotta mixture; it should make about 20 balls. Add the balls to the gently boiling water in four batches and cook 4 to 5 minutes, turning them occasionally, until just firm. Drain on paper towels and keep warm in a low oven while you cook the remaining dumplings.

4. Reheat the tomato sauce, if needed, and remove the basil sprigs. Serve the ricotta and wild greens dumplings on top of the tomato sauce with a sprinkling of extra basil.

Look out for **Good King Henry**, with its triangular leaves and spiky flowers, in rich soil or cultivated land. It's a generous plant, providing edible leaves pretty much all year round—though the smaller, younger leaves are preferable. The young stems are also edible, hence the plant's nickname of poor man's asparagus. In the home garden it is low maintenance and largely pest resistant.

To grow garlic, split a bulb into cloves. Plant the cloves, pointed end up, ½ inch deep and 4½ inches apart in pots or free-draining soil in late fall. Feed and water when dry throughout the growing season. Remove any flower heads; like onion or chive flowers these are edible, too. It is ready for harvesting when the leaves start to wilt and turn yellow. Eat fresh or let dry in a cool, dry place.

If you have a loaf of bread that is just past its best, avoid throwing it away by using it in this savory, cheesy bread pudding. Ideally, the loaf should have a slightly open-textured crumb so it absorbs the cheese and egg mixture and doesn't become too dense when baked. Don't ditch the crusts; they can be turned into breadcrumbs and frozen until you need them. Feel free to replace the cheddar with whatever cheese you have in the refrigerator, or try a mixture of different ones.

Cheese and Pepper Strata

Serves: 4   *Preparation time:* 15 minutes, plus 10 minutes standing
Cooking time: 1 hour

1 red bell pepper, seeded and sliced
1 yellow bell pepper, seeded and sliced
2 tablespoons olive oil
13 ounces slightly stale, open-textured bread,
    crusts removed, sliced and cut into squares
2 garlic cloves, crushed
6 scallions, sliced

1 large handful of basil leaves
2 cups sharp cheddar or cheese of choice,
    coarsely grated
6 eggs, lightly beaten
1¼ cups milk
sea salt and freshly ground black pepper

1. Preheat the oven to 350°F. Brush the peppers with the oil. Heat a large grill pan over high heat and grill the peppers 6 to 8 minutes, turning occasionally, until tender and starting to blacken in places. You may need to grill the peppers in batches.

2. Meanwhile, put half the bread in a large, shallow ovenproof dish. Top the bread with an even layer of cooked pepper, garlic, scallions, basil and half the cheddar.

3. Whisk together the eggs and milk and season with salt and pepper. Pour half the mixture into the dish, making sure the bread is evenly covered. Top with the remaining bread and pour the rest of the egg and milk mixture over it, pressing the bread down so it is thoroughly soaked. Scatter the remaining cheese over the top and let stand 10 minutes. Bake 35 to 40 minutes until the cheese has melted and is golden on top.

To extend the life of store-bought pots of fresh herbs during the warmer months, plant in larger pots or in the garden, then water regularly and wait for the new growth.

If you find beets with the stems and leaves still intact, they make a good alternative to chard, cavolo nero or spinach. Use them promptly and discard any that are damaged or wrinkly. I've splashed out on Gruyère cheese, but you could use sharp cheddar or crumbly goat or sheep cheese instead.

Beet Top, Scallion and Gruyère Tart

Serves: *4–6*   **Preparation time:** *20 minutes, plus making the pastry*
Cooking time: *1 hour 10 minutes*

butter, for greasing
1 recipe quantity Dough Pastry
   (see page 13)
all-purpose flour, for dusting

FILLING
1 tablespoon sunflower oil
2 bunches of scallions, sliced,
   green and white parts kept separate

tops from 4 large raw beets, stems and leaves
   thinly sliced and separated
1 handful of wild garlic leaves (see page 55)
   or chives, roughly chopped
3 large eggs, lightly beaten
1 cup whole milk
1 cup Gruyère (or Swiss) cheese,
   coarsely grated
sea salt and freshly ground black pepper

1. Preheat the oven to 375°F and heat a cookie sheet. Grease an 11-inch quiche dish.

2. Roll the dough out on a lightly floured work surface until about ¼ inch thick. Use the dough to line the prepared quiche dish, leaving a slight overhang. Line the pie shell with foil and baking beans. Put the quiche dish on the preheated cookie sheet and bake 15 minutes. Remove the foil and beans and return the quiche dish to the oven another 15 minutes until the pie shell is cooked and light golden.

3. Meanwhile, make the filling. Heat the oil in a large skillet over medium heat. Add the white part of the scallions and the beet stems and cook 2 minutes until tender. Add the green part of the scallions, beet leaves and wild garlic (if using chives, stir them into the egg and milk mixture, see below) and cook another 2 minutes until just softened.

4. Whisk together the eggs and milk in a bowl and season with salt and pepper. Spoon the scallion mixture into the pie shell and scatter the cheese over it in an even layer. Pour in the egg mixture, then return to the oven 40 minutes until the filling is just set. Serve cut into wedges.

Use dried beans if you don't have baking beans—soybeans are good. They can be reused, too—let them cool and store in an airtight container until the next time.

Beets

make an attractive addition to a vegetable bed. Sow the seeds in drills about ¾ inch deep and cover with compost. Water the soil and thin out the seedlings when they're about 1 inch tall, leaving a 4½-inch gap between them. The beets will be ready to harvest in about 3 months. Don't throw the leaves away, as they are delicious cooked and eaten like chard or spinach.

This always goes down well at home. It's like macaroni and cheese but with a lighter, stock-based cheese sauce, rather than a milky one. Shells are are perfect for capturing cheesy or creamy sauces, but you could use any type of short-cut, dried pasta you have in the cupboard.

Shells and Broccoli Gratin

Serves: *4*   **Preparation time:** *20 minutes, plus making the stock*
Cooking time: *30 minutes*

11½ ounces dried shells
1 large head of broccoli, thick stem removed,
    cut into small florets
2½ cups Vegetable Stock (see page 14)
½ cup whipping cream
2 tablespoons butter
2 large garlic cloves, finely chopped

2 tablespoons all-purpose flour
2 teaspoons Dijon mustard
5½-ounce mixture of hard cheeses,
    such as Gruyère (or Swiss) and sharp
    cheddar, coarsely grated
¼ cup day-old breadcrumbs
sea salt and freshly ground black pepper

1. Preheat the oven to 350°F. Cook the pasta in plenty of boiling salted water, following the package instructions, until al dente. Three minutes before the pasta is ready, add the broccoli florets to the pot. Drain the pasta and broccoli and tip them into a large, shallow casserole dish.

2. Meanwhile, bring the stock to a boil in a separate pan and boil gently until reduced slightly—to about 2 cups; this will help to concentrate its flavor. Remove from the heat and stir in the cream.

3. Melt the butter in a heavy pan over medium-low heat. Add the garlic and cook 1 minute until softened. Stir in the flour with a wooden spoon and cook 1 minute, then gradually mix in the stock mixture, stirring continuously to make a sauce the consistency of thin custard. Add the mustard and three quarters of the cheese, and season with salt and pepper.

4. Pour the sauce over the pasta and broccoli in the casserole dish and turn until everything is combined. Sprinkle the remaining cheese and breadcrumbs over it and bake 15 to 20 minutes until golden and crisp on top.

Keep the thick broccoli stalk for use in another recipe. Peel and cut into slices to add to stir-fries, soups, and stews.

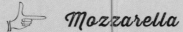 ## Mozzarella

A trip to an Italian delicatessen will reveal porcelain-white balls of mozzarella in a stunning range of shapes and sizes floating in tubs of whey or water. Mozzarella ranges from the single-bite globes known as bocconcini to the larger, cream-filled balls of burrata, and much more in between. Star of the show is mozzarella di bufala Campana (D.O.P.), made with buffalo milk using a protected, age-old method. In fact, all mozzarella was once made with buffalo milk, but cow's milk is now most common. This southern Italian fresh, unripened cheese with a milky, slightly sour edge and elastic texture is equally happy used as a main ingredient in classic salads—such as insalata Caprese, when it is combined with tomato and basil—as it is in a cooked dish, such as melanzane alla Parmigiana (baked layers of eggplant, tomato, mozzarella and parmesan); its unique melting properties also make it a must-have topping on a pizza.

Full of summer flavors, this roasted vegetable, mozzarella and croûton panzanella is a twist on the classic uncooked Italian salad. It's perfect for using up a glut of summer veg and calls for young, fresh cloves of garlic.

Roasted Panzanella

Serves: 4–6   Preparation time: 20 minutes   Cooking time: 40 minutes

¼ cup olive oil

2 red bell peppers, cut in half and seeded, each half cut into 3 wedges

2 yellow bell peppers, cut in half and seeded, each half cut into 3 wedges

2 red onions, cut in half and cut into wedges

2 zucchini, cut into ½-inch diagonal slices

6 vine-ripened tomatoes, seeded and quartered

6 garlic cloves, 2 peeled and 4 unpeeled

1 loaf day-old ciabatta or other crusty bread, cut in half lengthwise, then halved again crosswise

½ teaspoon cumin seeds

1 handful each of basil and oregano leaves

7 ounces mozzarella cheese, drained and torn into bite-size pieces

sea salt and freshly ground black pepper

DRESSING

¼ cup extra virgin olive oil

3 tablespoons balsamic vinegar

1. Preheat the oven to 400°F. Put the olive oil in a large bowl and add the peppers, onions, zucchini and tomatoes, season with salt and pepper, and turn to coat everything in the oil. Tip the vegetables into two large roasting pans and spread out in an even layer. Add the 4 unpeeled garlic cloves and roast 20 minutes, or until the garlic is very soft. Remove the garlic and tomatoes from the roasting pans and set to one side. Turn the rest of the vegetables in the pans and return them to the oven for 20 minutes more until tender and slightly browned around the edges.

2. Meanwhile, heat a large grill pan over medium heat. Grill the ciabatta 6 minutes, turning once, until toasted and blackened in places. Cut the remaining peeled garlic in half, rub the cut half over the toasted ciabatta and let cool.

3. To make the dressing, put the ingredients in a jar and season with salt and pepper. Squeeze the roasted garlic out of its papery shell and finely chop. Add the garlic to the dressing, cover and shake well until combined. Put the roasted vegetables on a large serving plate. Tear the ciabatta into bite-size pieces and scatter them over the top along with the cumin seeds, herbs and mozzarella. Spoon the dressing over it and serve.

Pictured on page 149.

▶▶ Scamorza, Orzo and Basil Oil Salad

I'm generally not a fan of pasta salads, but this is something else. Scamorza, a form of smoked mozzarella with a firmer texture, is delicious cubed and stirred into **2 cups cooked orzo** pasta. About **5½ ounces scamorza** will do. Add **2 small sliced avocados, 3 seeded and chopped tomatoes** and **2 handfuls of arugula leaves**. For the dressing, blend ⅓ **cup extra virgin olive oil** with **3 handfuls of basil leaves, 1 garlic clove, the juice of 1 large lemon** and **salt** and **pepper** until combined. Spoon it over the salad and toss until combined. Scatter over it **2 tablespoons toasted pine nuts** (see page 18) to serve.

▶▶ Chinese Black Bean and Mozzarella Salad

A clash of cultures maybe, but this works so well. Soak **3 tablespoons Chinese fermented black beans** in just-boiled water 20 minutes, then drain (save the stock for another recipe). Meanwhile, mix together **2 tablespoons sunflower oil, 1 teaspoon sesame oil** and **2 teaspoons light soy sauce** in a bowl. Stir in **1 finely chopped scallion, ½ chopped and seeded red chili, 1 teaspoon peeled and finely chopped ginger root** and the drained black beans. Put **10½ ounces drained and thickly sliced mozzarella cheese** in a bowl and spoon the dressing over the top. Scatter over it **1 handful each of chopped cilantro and basil leaves**.

▶▶ Mozzarella with Szechuan Pepper

A warm salad with a mouth-tingling dressing: toast **1 teaspoon Szechuan peppercorns** in a large, dry skillet 1 minute until aromatic. Remove from the pan and grind with ½ **teaspoon sea salt**. Add **2 tablespoons olive oil** to the pan and fry **2 diagonally-sliced golden zucchini** 5 minutes, or until tender and starting to color. Transfer to a serving plate along with any juices in the pan and scatter over **5½ ounces mozzarella cheese**, torn into pieces. Sprinkle with as much of the Szechuan salt as you like.

Chapter 7
Box of Veg

Vegetables offer an almost infinite number of culinary possibilities to the home cook and are much, much more than just a side dish. The recipes in this chapter will open your eyes to new possibilities, from the stunning Potato and Borage Salad, to golden, crisp Pea and Tofu Fritters, and aromatic Moroccan Slow-Cooked Vegetables. When it comes to buying vegetables, seasonal is best; not only will they be kinder on the purse, they'll taste better too. That said, don't forget the ultimate convenience food—frozen veg.

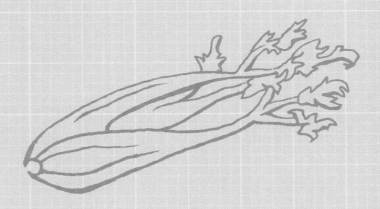

Cornflower-blue, star-shaped borage flowers look attractive and have a fresh taste reminiscent of cucumber—and what's more, the leaves of this annual herb are edible too. I also like to add a handful of finely chopped wild or cultivated sorrel leaves to the salad dressing in place of the lemon zest. It has a citrusy sharpness that works well with creamy sauces and resembles young, pointed spinach leaves. Find it on grassland and along banks from spring to late fall.

Potato and Borage Salad

Serves: *4*   **Preparation time:** *15 minutes*   **Cooking time:** *16 minutes*

1½ pounds new potatoes, scrubbed and cut in
   half if large
4 eggs
1 handful of borage flowers and young leaves,
   leaves shredded
1 small red onion, cut into rings
10 radishes, thinly sliced
2 tablespoons extra virgin olive oil
1 small handful of wild fennel fronds or dill,
   chopped
sea salt and freshly ground black pepper

LEMON CREAM
½ cup lowfat plain yogurt
2 tablespoons mayonnaise
juice and finely grated zest of 1 small lemon
2 teaspoons wholegrain mustard

Serve with the Easter Egg Pies (see page 120).

1. Put the potatoes in a large pot, cover with water and bring to a boil over medium-high heat. Turn the heat down slightly, add the eggs to the pot, part-cover with a lid and gently boil 6 minutes. Remove the eggs, cool them under cold running water and set to one side. Continue to cook the potatoes for another 10 minutes, or until tender. Drain well.

2. Meanwhile, mix together the ingredients for the lemon cream along with 2 tablespoons water, season with salt and pepper and set to one side.

3. Cut the potatoes into bite-size pieces and place in a serving bowl along with the borage leaves. Scatter the red onion and radishes over them, drizzle the oil over the top and turn lightly until combined. Drizzle over them half of the lemon cream.

4. Peel and roughly mash the eggs, then pile them on top of the potatoes. Scatter the fennel fronds and borage flowers over them. Serve the salad with the remaining lemon cream on the side.

Borage is an annual herb that blooms from spring onwards, prolonged with regular deadheading. It is self-seeding, often found growing wild, and also makes an attractive garden plant. Pollinating bees love it, so it is a good companion to tomatoes and strawberries. Both the flowers and young leaves are edible but the latter (as well as the stems) can become prickly later on in the season.

This main-meal salad takes all the elements of the classic Lebanese fattoush but gives it a Mexican twist—so there are toasted corn tortillas, chunks of avocado, tangy lime juice and lots of fresh cilantro. It's best dressed just before serving so the toasted tortillas remain crisp, and at room temperature to let the flavors sing through.

Mexican Fattoush

Serves: 4   Preparation time: 15 minutes   Cooking time: 16 minutes

2 soft corn tortillas
5 large vine-ripened tomatoes, seeded and cut
   into chunks
1 large yellow bell pepper, seeded and cut
   into chunks
1 small red onion, thinly sliced into rings
2 avocados, pitted, peeled and cut into chunks
1 handful of cilantro leaves, chopped
1 handful of mint leaves, chopped

1 red chili, seeded and freshly chopped
  (optional)

DRESSING
3 tablespoons extra virgin olive oil, plus extra
  for brushing
juice of 1 lime
sea salt and freshly ground black pepper

1. Lightly brush both sides of each tortilla with olive oil. Heat a large, nonstick skillet over medium-low heat and toast the tortillas, one at a time, 3 to 4 minutes, turning once, until crisp on both sides. Let cool and crisp up a bit more, then tear them up roughly.

2. Put the tomatoes, yellow bell pepper, onion and avocados in a shallow serving bowl, then scatter the herbs over the top.

3. Mix together the ingredients for the dressing and season with salt and pepper. Pour the dressing over the salad and toss gently until combined. Scatter the toasted tortillas and chili (if using) over the top, toss again and serve immediately.

To keep a year-round supply of fresh herbs, remove the leaves from their stalks and freeze the leaves—chopped or whole—spread out in a single layer on a baking sheet. The stalks can be frozen separately and ground or finely chopped for use in soups and stews. You can also freeze fresh herbs in ice cube trays suspended in a little water.

Great served with the Semolina and Nut Milk Gnocchi (see page 96), this dish is highly adaptable, making a delicious topping on bruschetta, served with pasta or rice for a more substantial meal, or as part of a selection of mezes. It will keep in the fridge up to 3 days, but is best served at room temperature or warm.

Eggplant Meze

Serves: 4   *Preparation time:* 10 minutes   *Cooking time:* 20 minutes

⅓ cup olive oil
1 large eggplant, cubed
4 garlic cloves, finely chopped
1½-inch piece of root ginger, peeled
   and finely grated
1 teaspoon cumin seeds

2 teaspoons ground coriander
1 teaspoon turmeric
3 tomatoes, seeded and chopped
juice of 1 lemon
sea salt and freshly ground black pepper

1. Heat the olive oil in a large, nonstick skillet over medium heat. Add the eggplant and fry 10 minutes, turning occasionally, until golden all over and tender. Stir in the garlic, ginger and cumin seeds and cook another minute until the garlic has softened.

2. Add the spices, tomatoes and ⅓ cup water and bring to a gentle boil, then turn the heat down and simmer 10 minutes, stirring occasionally, until reduced and thickened. Remove from the heat, stir in the lemon juice and season with salt and pepper. Serve warm or at room temperature.

It's no longer necessary to salt eggplants before you use them to extract the bitter juices, because over the years any bitterness has been bred out of them. However, salting does curb the amount of oil the eggplant absorbs when fried.

This dish of braised summer vegetables has a Moroccan feel with the tangy preserved lemons, olives and spices. I like to serve the vegetables with crisp slices of grilled polenta (see page 86), but steamed couscous is good, too.

Moroccan Slow-Cooked Vegetables

Serves: 4–6   *Preparation time:* 15 minutes, plus making the preserved lemons and 15 minutes soaking   *Cooking time:* 55 minutes

⅓ cup sundried tomatoes, thickly sliced

2 teaspoons Poor Man's Saffron (see page 76) or a large pinch of saffron

3 tablespoons olive oil

1 large onion, sliced

2 large fennel bulbs, fronds trimmed and reserved, cut in half lengthwise and cut into ½-inch wedges

3 zucchini, cut into large bite-size chunks

1 cup small black pitted olives

1 teaspoon turmeric

1 teaspoon vegetable bouillon powder

2 tablespoons thyme leaves

1 teaspoon dried thyme

1 recipe quantity Quick Preserved Lemons (see page 24)

sea salt and freshly ground black pepper

1 recipe quantity Polenta Bruschetta (see page 86), to serve

1. Soak the sundried tomatoes and Poor Man's Saffron in 1¾ cups hot water for 15 minutes.

2. Meanwhile, heat the olive oil in a large, heavy pot over medium-low heat. Add the onion and cook, covered, 10 minutes, stirring occasionally, until softened. Add the fennel and cook another 5 minutes until starting to soften.

3. Add the zucchini, olives and sundried tomatoes along with their saffron soaking water and bring to a boil. Stir in the turmeric, bouillon powder and thyme, turn the heat down to low and simmer, part-covered, 30 minutes, stirring occasionally. Add the preserved lemons and cook, uncovered, another 10 minutes until the sauce has reduced and thickened and the vegetables are tender. Season with salt and pepper, and serve with the Polenta Bruschetta, sprinkled with reserved fennel fronds.

Olives are also used in the Paella with Poor Man's Saffron (see page 76).

It's worth harvesting wild fennel flowers for use in the kitchen or for planting next year. Put a small paper bag over the flower head, secure with a rubber band, hang upside down and leave for a few weeks in a cool, dry place. When dry, shake the flower heads to remove the seeds.

This makes a light, summery meal or appetizer. After cooking the fava beans, it's best to remove their gray outer peel, which can be tough, to reveal the tender green bean inside. The peeled beans are then stirred into a lemony goat cheese mousse with some chopped kohlrabi. I'd shied away from the alien-looking kohlrabi until fairly recently, but I'm pleasantly surprised at how good it tastes—like a cross between a radish and a turnip—with a fresh, crisp texture.

Fava Bean and Goat Cheese Crostini

Serves: 4   **Preparation time:** 15 minutes, plus making the Quick Preserved Lemons (optional)   **Cooking time:** 10 minutes

4 cups shelled fava beans
½ cup peeled and chopped kohlrabi
1 handful of mint leaves, chopped
8 thick slices of country-style bread/ciabatta
1 large garlic clove, cut in half
½ small red onion, thinly sliced

GOAT CHEESE MOUSSE
8 ounces fresh, mild goat cheese
2 teaspoons finely chopped Quick Preserved Lemons (see page 24), or zest of 1 lemon
2 tablespoons milk
2 tablespoons olive oil
sea salt and freshly ground black pepper

1. Bring a pot of salted water to a boil over high heat. Add the fava beans and boil gently 2 to 3 minutes until tender, then drain and refresh under cold running water. When cool, peel off the gray outer skins and put the peeled beans in a bowl along with the kohlrabi and half of the mint.

2. While the beans are cooking, make the goat cheese mousse. Beat together the goat cheese, preserved lemons, milk and olive oil, then season with salt and pepper. Fold into the fava bean mixture.

3. Toast the bread and rub one side of each slice with the cut side of the garlic. Serve the toast topped with the fava bean mixture and scatter the onion and remaining mint over them.

Use leftover herbs to make herbal tea infusions: mint, fennel, nettle, lemon balm and lemon verbena are particularly good.

Kohlrabi

is a brassica with a swollen, bulb-like root that grows above ground and has thick, leafy stalks. It is a fast grower, taking about 10 weeks from seed until harvest. Both the bulb and the leaves are edible: serve the former grated into salads or lightly sautéed in butter; the leaves can be served like cabbage. Look for the purple variety, which will add glorious color to the garden.

These Oriental-inspired fritters come with my take on the Japanese ponzu dipping sauce, which is a sweet-sour-salty combination of citrus juice, soy sauce and brown sugar.

Pea and Tofu Fritters

Serves: 4　*Preparation time:* 20 minutes　*Cooking time:* 25 minutes

7 ounces firm tofu, drained, patted dry and coarsely grated

heaped 1¼ cups fresh shelled or frozen peas, defrosted if frozen

6 scallions, finely chopped

2 large garlic cloves, crushed

1-inch piece of ginger root, grated (no need to peel)

½ teaspoon dried red pepper flakes

¾ cup plus 1½ tablespoons all-purpose flour

3 eggs, lightly beaten

1 scant cup sunflower oil

sea salt and freshly ground black pepper

4 handfuls of pea shoots, to serve

PONZU DIPPING SAUCE

⅓ cup light soy sauce or tamari

⅓ cup fresh orange juice

2 tablespoons lemon juice or rice vinegar

4 teaspoons light brown sugar

1. Squeeze the grated tofu in a clean lintfree dish towel to remove any excess water and tip into a bowl along with the peas, 5 of the chopped scallions, and the garlic, ginger and red pepper flakes and mix together.

2. Put the flour in a separate bowl, make a well in the center and add the beaten eggs. Gradually mix the eggs into the flour until you have a thick, smooth batter, then stir in the pea mixture and season well with salt and pepper.

3. Heat the oil in a large, deep skillet over medium heat. Spoon heaped tablespoons of the batter into the pan and cook 5 to 6 fritters at a time 3 to 4 minutes on each side until golden. Drain on paper towels and keep warm in a low oven while you cook the remaining fritters; it should make about 16 in total.

4. Meanwhile, mix together all the ingredients for the ponzu dipping sauce and season with pepper. Divide the sauce between four bowls and sprinkle with the remaining chopped scallion. Top the fritters with a handful of pea shoots and serve with the dipping sauce.

Serve with the Soba, Seaweed and Radish Salad (see page 65).

Plump and sweet, young *peas* are delicious eaten straight from the pod or cooked lightly. Plant seeds outdoors in spring, in a sunny position. Plant taller growing plants in nutrient-rich soil in a single row, 2 inches deep, making sure there is enough room for cane supports. Dwarf plants can be sown in a round trench. Harvest the peas regularly or the plants will stop producing flowers and pods.

I prefer to mash the kidney beans to give a chunky texture to the bean patties. You could use a food processor for a smoother end result, but bear in mind that canned beans are softer in texture than beans cooked from dried. The chipotle paste, made from smoked jalapeño chilies, is a favorite and adds a rich, smoky, spicy kick. To complement the Mexican feel, try serving the bean patties with the Mexican Fattoush (see page 187).

Chipotle, Carrot & Red Bean Patties

Serves: *4*   **Preparation time:** *20 minutes*   **Cooking time:** *12 minutes*

3 cups drained canned red kidney beans or cooked dried beans (see pages 8–9)
1 large carrot, coarsely grated
3 garlic cloves, crushed
1 handful of micro sprouts, such as radish, alfalfa or broccoli
1½ cups fresh breadcrumbs
2 to 3 tablespoons tomato ketchup, to taste
2 to 3 tablespoons smoked chipotle paste, to taste

flour, for dusting
vegetable oil, for frying
1 large handful of cilantro leaves, chopped, to serve

SWEET CHILI AND LIME YOGURT
½ cup thick plain yogurt
juice of 1 lime
¼ cup sweet chili sauce, or to taste
sea salt and freshly ground black pepper

1. To make the sweet chili and lime yogurt, mix together all the ingredients in a serving bowl and season with salt and pepper.

2. Mash the kidney beans with a fork or potato masher in a bowl to make a coarse paste. Stir in the carrot, garlic, micro sprouts, breadcrumbs, ketchup and chipotle paste. Season well with salt and pepper, then taste and add more chipotle if you like more of a kick. Alternatively, add an extra tablespoon of ketchup.

3. Dust a large plate with flour. Form the bean mixture into 12 patties (or 4 large burgers) about ⅝ inch thick. Dust lightly with flour, patting the patties to remove any excess.

4. Heat enough oil to cover the bottom of a large, nonstick skillet over medium heat. Fry the bean patties in two batches 3 minutes on each side, or until golden and crisp. Drain on paper towels and keep warm. Serve the bean patties with the sweet chili and lime yogurt, sprinkled with cilantro.

Root vegetables cost little to buy and add nourishment and substance to this warming, filling pie.

Winter Root, Cheddar & Cider Pie

Serves: 4–6   *Preparation time:* 45 minutes, plus cooling
Cooking time: 50 minutes

4 turnips, chopped
2 parsnips, chopped
3 carrots,chopped
1¾ cups celery root, chopped
1 tablespoon vegetable bouillon powder
1½ tablespoons butter
2 onions, chopped
7 ounces crimini mushrooms, sliced
4 garlic cloves, chopped
leaves of 6 thyme sprigs, or 1 teaspoon
    dried thyme

1 heaped tablespoon chopped sage leaves,
    plus 3 large leaves
2 heaped tablespoons flour, plus extra
    for dusting
1 cup hard cider
1 tablespoon Dijon mustard
1⅔ cup sharp cheddar cheese, grated
14 ounces puff pastry dough
1 egg, beaten, to glaze
sea salt and freshly ground black pepper

1. Put the root vegetables in a large pot and just cover with water. Bring to a boil and stir in the bouillon powder. Turn the heat down, part-cover and simmer 12 to 15 minutes until the vegetables are tender. Strain the vegetables, reserving the stock.

2. Meanwhile, melt the butter in a large skillet over medium-high heat and fry the onions 8 minutes until softened. Add the mushrooms, garlic and herbs and cook another 5 minutes. Sprinkle the flour over the top and stir continuously another minute. Pour in the cider, stir to lift any bits from the bottom of the skillet and cook 2 minutes until thickened and reduced. Add the cooked root vegetables, 1½ cups of the reserved stock, and the mustard and stir until combined. Season the filling well with salt and pepper. Transfer the root vegetable mixture to an 11-inch deep baking dish, round or square, and preferably with a lip. Stir in the cheese and let cool.

3. Preheat the oven to 400°F. Roll out the dough on a lightly floured counter until large enough to cover the baking dish with about 1 inch to spare. Cut a ½-inch-wide strip from the edge. Wet the rim of the baking dish with water and top with the strip of dough. Brush the top of the strip with more water and drape the rolled-out dough on top. Press the edge of the pie dough to seal, trim away any excess dough and crimp with your finger and thumb. Tap the edge of the pastry with the flat blade of a table knife. Prick the top of the pie dough and brush the top with beaten egg. Arrange the sage leaves on top and brush with a little more egg. Bake 30 minutes until risen and golden. Serve hot.

Saltado is a Peruvian one-pan dish with an Asian influence. Traditionally made with beef, this meat-free version features marinated cubes of tofu, new potatoes and red bell peppers in a herby, spicy tomato sauce.

Pepper and Tofu Saltado

Serves: 4 *Preparation time:* 20 minutes, plus 1 hour marinating
Cooking time: 45 minutes

⅓ cup dark soy sauce

3 heaped teaspoons hot chili paste

14 ounces firm tofu, drained, patted dry and
   cut into cubes

3 tablespoons olive oil, plus extra if needed

1 pound new potatoes, peeled and cubed

2 large onions, chopped

2 large red bell peppers, seeded and
   cut into chunks

4 large garlic cloves, crushed

2 teaspoons ground coriander

2 teaspoons ground cumin

1 tablespoon white wine vinegar

1¼ pounds tomatoes, skinned,
   seeded and chopped

2 large handfuls of mint leaves, chopped

2 large handfuls of coriander leaves, chopped

1. Mix together 2 tablespoons of the soy sauce and 2 teaspoons of the chili paste in a large, shallow dish. Add the tofu and turn until it is coated in the marinade. Let marinate 1 hour.

2. Twenty minutes before the tofu is ready, heat the oil in a large, deep skillet over medium heat. Add the potatoes and fry 16 to 18 minutes, turning regularly, until golden and crisp all over. Remove the potatoes with a slotted spoon and drain on paper towels. Add the tofu to the skillet and cook 10 minutes, turning occasionally, until golden all over. Remove from the pan and drain on paper towels.

3. Add more oil to the skillet if needed, then add the onion and cook 6 minutes until softened. Add the red bell peppers and cook another 3 minutes until tender. While they are cooking, mix together the garlic, ground spices, vinegar and the remaining soy sauce and chili paste, then add it to the pan with the tomatoes and ⅓ cup water. Cook 5 minutes, stirring regularly, until the tomatoes break down to make a sauce. Return the cooked potatoes and tofu to the pan along with three quarters of the herbs and heat through. Serve sprinkled with the remaining herbs.

A jar of harissa goes a long way in my kitchen. It's spooned into mayo to make a quick sauce, brushed over roasted vegetables and stirred into couscous or, as here, used as the base of a quick marinade. The mushroom burgers come topped with a slice of golden grilled halloumi and a spoonful of red bell pepper and cumin dressing.

Mushroom Burgers

Serves: 4   **Preparation time:** 10 minutes, plus 30 minutes marinating
Cooking time: 12 minutes

3 tablespoons extra virgin olive oil
1 tablespoon harissa
1 teaspoon lemon juice
4 large, flat portobello or field mushrooms,
  stalks discarded
4 slices of halloumi, rinsed and patted dry
4 focaccia rolls, split in half
sea salt and freshly ground black pepper
green salad, to serve

RED BELL PEPPER AND CUMIN DRESSING
2 tablespoons extra virgin olive oil
½ large red bell pepper, seeded and cubed
1 large garlic clove, finely chopped
½ teaspoon cumin seeds
1 tablespoon balsamic vinegar
2 heaped tablespoons roughly chopped
  cilantro leaves

1. Mix together the olive oil, harissa and lemon juice and season with salt and pepper. Brush the marinade generously over both sides of each mushroom and let marinate 30 minutes.

2. Preheat the broiler to medium-high, and make the red bell pepper and cumin dressing. Heat 1 tablespoon of the oil in a large skillet over medium heat. Add the red bell pepper and fry 3 minutes until softened, then add the garlic and cumin seeds and cook another minute, stirring regularly. Remove from the heat and transfer to a small bowl. Stir in the remaining oil, balsamic vinegar and cilantro, then season with salt and pepper. Set to one side.

3. Put the marinated mushrooms, gill sides down, on a sheet of foil. Fold in the edges to make a border and to keep in any juices. Broil for 5 minutes until softened, then turn over and broil for another minute. Turn the broiler to high, place a slice of halloumi on top of each mushroom and broil another 2 to 3 minutes until softened and golden in places.

4. Broil the focaccia at the same time as cooking the mushrooms, until lightly toasted. To serve, put a halloumi-topped mushroom on the bottom half of each focaccia and top with a generous spoonful of the dressing. Spoon any of the juices from the broiled mushrooms over the other half of the focaccia and place it on top of the mushrooms. Serve with a green salad.

Only *pick mushrooms* when you are absolutely sure what they are. Arm yourself with a guidebook or, even better, attend a course or go with a seasoned forager. The field mushroom is perhaps the most commonly eaten wild fungus. Find them in meadows, fields and pastureland from late summer into fall. Take care when identifying them, as there are poisonous fungi that look very like them.

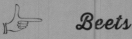 # Beets

Out of the many vegetables to choose from it may seem strange to pick beets, but their earthy, sweet flavor and vibrant magenta color means they lend themselves to so many savory — and even sweet — dishes. Beets are a close relative of chard and spinach, so be sure not to waste the leaves, as they can be prepared and cooked in the same way. Bake the firm beet globes whole (unpeeled to stop them bleeding) or reduce the roasting time by cutting them into wedges; either way they need to be cooked until tender and richly sweet. Alternatively, boil, pickle or grate raw into salads — and cakes! And then there's the stunning Italian candy-striped beets, also known as chioggia, with their concentric circles in varying shades of pink, red, yellow and white. They look dramatic cut into paper-thin slices and served as part of a salad.

Adding beets to savory or sweet muffins makes them wonderfully moist, in much the same way as adding carrots or zucchini does, and they also benefit from the vegetable's vibrant ruby color. If using ready-cooked beets, make sure you buy the kind without any vinegar. Also, try to use a crumbly goat cheese rather than a runny one for the best results. The secret to successful light muffins is to keep mixing to a minimum; briefly fold the ingredients together and you're done—they don't even have to be thoroughly combined.

Beet and Goat Cheese Muffins

Makes: 12   **Preparation time:** 15 minutes   **Cooking time:** 25 minutes

sunflower oil, for greasing
2 cups plus 2 tablespoons all-purpose flour
½ teaspoon sea salt
2 teaspoons baking powder
½ teaspoon baking soda
2 large eggs, lightly beaten

1¼ cups plain yogurt
⅓ cup plus 2 teaspoons butter, melted
4 ounces goat cheese, crumbled (about 1 cup)
8 ounces cooked beets, coarsely grated
 (about 1⅔ cups)
2 tablespoons pumpkin seeds

1. Preheat the oven to 375°F. Lightly grease a 12-cup deep muffin pan with oil (or you could make 6 large muffins using large paper muffin cups in a large muffin-pan).

2. Sift together the flour, salt, baking powder and baking soda into a mixing bowl.

3. Mix together the eggs and yogurt and beat in the melted butter. Stir the dry ingredients into the wet ingredients, then gently fold in the goat cheese and beets until just combined. Spoon the mixture into the prepared muffin pan, sprinkle with the pumpkin seeds and bake 20 to 25 minutes, or until risen and golden.

Rather than waste the leftover egg whites, freeze them in a small plastic carton or ice cube tray. Save them up and use to make meringues or for the base of a tempura batter.

Pictured on page 171.

►► Beet Jam

A spoonful of this thick, sticky, earthy, savory jam goes particularly well with robust-flavored cheeses, or nut or bean-based dishes. Sauté **1 large finely chopped onion** in **1 tablespoon olive oil** 10 minutes until softened but not colored. Add **2 (about 10 ounces) peeled and grated raw beets**, **1 large peeled and grated apple**, **½ cup cider vinegar**, **½ cup water** and **¼ cup brown sugar**. Stir well and bring to a boil, then turn the heat down to medium-low, part-cover the pan and simmer 40 minutes until the beets are very tender. Remove the lid and simmer 15 minutes, stirring now and then, to reduce the liquid in the pan and until the mixture is jam-like in consistency. Season with **salt** and **pepper** and let the jam cool before serving, or spoon into a sterilized jar (see page 11) and keep for up to 1 month.

►► Lebanese Beet Dip

This simple dip is delicious slathered onto warm flatbreads or scooped up with vegetables. I like to roast my own beets, but you could use ready-cooked if time is short. Preheat the oven to 400°F. Trim **2 (about 10 ounces) beets** and wrap them in foil. Roast 1 hour to 1 hour 15 minutes until the beets can be easily pierced all the way through with a skewer. Leave them until cool enough to handle, then peel away the skin and roughly chop. Blend the beets with **⅓ cup plain yogurt**, **the juice of ½ lemon**, **1 crushed garlic clove**, **1 chopped red chili**, **2 teaspoons ras el hanout** and **½ teaspoon ground cumin** until smooth. Season well with **salt** and **pepper** and spoon the dip into a serving bowl. Serve scattered with **crumbled feta cheese** and **cilantro** and **mint leaves**.

►► Roast Beet Crisps

Preheat the oven to 350°F. Thinly slice **5 raw beets** (the slices should be about ⅛inch thick) using a mandolin or very sharp knife. Pat the beet slices dry with paper towels and lightly brush both sides with **olive oil**. Put in a single layer on two baking sheets and roast for 20 to 25 minutes, turning the beet slices once and swapping the trays around at the same time, until just crisp (they will crisp up more when cool). Keep an eye on the beets as they can burn easily in a matter of minutes. Drain on paper towels and season with **sea salt**.

Index

ACKNOWLEDGMENTS

My heartfelt thanks go to Grace Cheetham, for her ongoing support, encouragement and belief in me. It has—as always—been an utmost pleasure to work with the dedicated team at Nourish, especially Rebecca Woods and Suzanne Tuhrim, who have been fantastic. I would also like to thank my freelance editor, Liz Jones. Thanks, too, to Jayne Cross who prepared the food for photography and brought the recipes to life, as did the talented (and funny) photographer, Toby Scott, and stylist Lucy Harvey. It was great to work with you all. I would also like to thank Silvio, Ella and Joel for putting up with the mess I always seem to make—and for happily tasting my creations, even late into the evening!

NOURISH
EAT WELL, LIVE WELL

Few things in life are as important as what you eat.
If you've enjoyed this book and want to read more about wholesome and healthy food,
please visit us at **www.nourishbooks.com**